The Baring Securities
Guide to International
Financial Reporting

The Baring Securities
Guide to International
Financial Reporting

Christopher Nobes

B BLACKWELL
Finance

First published 1991

Basil Blackwell Ltd
108 Cowley Road, Oxford, OX4 1JF, UK

Basil Blackwell, Inc.
3 Cambridge Center
Cambridge, Massachusetts 02142, USA

British Library Cataloguing in Publication Data
A CIP catalogue record for this book is available from the British Library.

Library of Congress Cataloging in Publication Data

Nobes, Christopher.
    The Baring Securities guide to international financial reporting/
Christopher Nobes.
      p. cm.
    Includes index.
    ISBN 0-631-17617-9
    1. International business enterprises—Accounting.
    2. International business enterprises—Accounting—Case studies.
    3. Financial statements.   I. Title.
    HF5686.I56N628 1991
    657'.3—dc20   90-47801
                                                    CIP

Typeset in 10 on 12 pt Helvetica by The Alden Press Ltd
Printed in Great Britain by The Alden Press Ltd.

CONTENTS

FOREWORD

One of the most significant developments in international financial markets in recent years has been the dramatic growth in cross-border equity investment. This has been prompted by increasing market efficiencies and greater competition within the financial services industry, which has forced investors to look beyond individual markets to enhance returns and reduce portfolio risk.

The growth in cross-border investment has been one of the key elements behind Baring Securities' rapid expansion since 1984. A major factor underlying the company's success has been the provision of a comprehensive range of products and services catering to the needs of the cross-border investor. Through its network of nineteen offices, Baring Securities services a global institutional client base in the markets of the Asia-Pacific region, Europe and Latin America.

The search for better returns from around the world has posed a crucial question to investment managers – how to identify value given different international accounting practices. Such differences make it difficult to compare directly equity investments around the globe.

A principal purpose of this book is to assist the global investor in the task of comparing and contrasting potential international investments. It sets out to relate the diverse accounting practices around the world to those which are considered normal in the US and Great Britain. In addition to highlighting the key areas of disparity, the book aims to enhance understanding of how these differences in practice arose.

A key feature is the analysis of the impact of 1992 on accounting standards around Europe. To date, harmonisation of accounting practices on the continent has progressed slowly. It is hoped that such differences will be gradually minimised, given the pressures to standardise across the board.

In order to simplify the task of reconciling accounts in the world's numerous financial markets, this book provides a number of case studies. These analyses are set out to aid investors' understanding of the key issues which arise when trying to compare the earnings and asset values of a range of international companies.

I hope that readers find this book an indispensable ally in their search for value in the international investment arena and that its publication demonstrates Baring Securities' continuing commitment to the demands of the cross-border investor.

Christopher Heath
Managing Director, Baring Securities

PREFACE

This book is intended for all those who use financial statements from more than one country: investors, lenders, analysts, bankers, managers, accountants, auditors and so on. The purpose is to illuminate the international differences in financial reporting and to begin to suggest methods of comparison.

Readers will know well that the financial world is changing very fast, and they should note that even while this book is being printed some aspects of it may become out of date. However, the book tries to stress longer-lasting principles and concepts, using individual country practices and company figures for illustrations.

I am most grateful for the initial encouragement and subsequent help of Christopher Hutton-Williams (agent), Tim Goodfellow (Basil Blackwell) and Andrew Baylis and colleagues (Baring Securities). In particular, it is the backing of Baring Securities that has made the book available in this attractive way.

During the preparation of this book, I have naturally drawn on my experience and previous writings in this area over the last fifteen years. Consequently, some parts of the book are expansions or précis or updated versions of ideas that I have expressed elsewhere. They have been tailored here with a precise purpose in mind. In this context, I acknowledge *Accountancy* and Professor S. Maeda concerning Chapter VII.

I should also acknowledge the word-processing skills of Meg Wells. Despite all the help that I have received from those mentioned here, I remain responsible for any errors or infelicities.

Christopher Nobes

I. SETTING THE SCENE

The commercial world is becoming increasingly internationalised. Many companies own subsidiaries in foreign countries and wish to buy more; financial institutions all around the world need to advise personal and corporate clients about investing in foreign companies; and markets are being globalised so that the same share can be traded on many different exchanges. For all these reasons, it is becoming vital to be able to:

- Know that accounting is enormously different from one country to another
- Understand the places to look for major differences
- Carry out corporate comparisons across frontiers.

The recent growing interest in currency union in Europe might lead some to suppose that one of the difficulties of international appraisal and investment may soon be solved. However, currency union, while useful, would have little impact on the difficulties caused by accounting differences, as this book will demonstrate.

Accounting has developed over many thousands of years. Developments have occurred when the complexity of commerce has made them relevant and useful. For example, increasing complexity of business in late medieval northern Italy led to the emergence of double entry; later, the existence of a wealthy merchant class and the need for large investment for major projects led to public subscription of share capital in seventeenth-century Holland; later still, the growing separation of ownership from management raised the need for audit in nineteenth-century Britain. Many countries have contributed: France led in the development of the profit and loss account; Germany gave us standardised formats for financial statements. From the late nineteenth century, the commercial power of the United States rose hand-in-hand with major developments in accounting, such as consolidation and many aspects of management accounting.

Although ideas spread from one culture to another, accounting has remained markedly different across countries because of this history and the different purposes that accounting serves. These differences have always been interesting, partly because they can teach us about how to improve our own system. However, now the differences are of major significance because of the internationalisation discussed above. This, of course, leads some interested parties to try to remove or reduce the differences. The European Community is notable for its efforts in this area.

The extraordinary political events of 1989 in Eastern Europe have led to enormous interest in investment opportunities there. However, as yet there is little publicly available financial reporting, so Eastern Europe cannot be considered in detail here.

This book examines the above problems by chapter as follows:

I. The types of problems to be encountered when dealing with foreign financial statements.

II. An investigation into the differences and similarities of US and UK accounting. From this basis, we go out into the rest of the world with a form of Anglo-American accounting as our benchmark in order to make comparisons.

III. The causes of international differences in financial reporting, including the variety of company types, stock exchanges, tax systems, legal systems and rule-makers. Countries are grouped by similarities and differences; this helps to illustrate the nature and depth of differences.

IV. An examination of the main practical ways in which the content of annual reports can differ. These are the areas that most need attention.

V. A discussion of consolidation and matters connected with it, such as segmental reporting and currency translation. This chapter takes a close look at the international problems in this particularly contentious area.

VI. A summary so far of the particular problems to be met when trying to make international comparisons, particularly of earnings and net assets.

VII. A study of Japan, in which many users of annual reports are particularly interested. Accounting there is sufficiently different from that in Europe and North America for it to make sense to discuss the country separately in this chapter.

VIII. The purposes, methods and progress of harmonisation of accounting worldwide and particularly in the EC. The International Accounting Standards Committee and the Directives of the EC are looked at in detail.

IX. A suggestion for a benchmark for international comparisons of company accounting data.

A glossary of common US and UK accounting terms is provided at the end of the book; equivalent terms in other languages are included. There is also a ready reference of accounting practices, country by country, for eleven major countries.

How things differ

This book examines a number of ways in which accounting differs internationally, and suggests ways of handling these problems. Differences include:

- Availability of published accounting data
- Language problems
- Extent and type of audit
- Formats of financial statements
- Frequency of reports
- Quantity of data disclosed
- Different currencies
- Biases in the accounting data
- User-friendliness of annual reports
- Valuation of assets
- Measurement of profits
- Cultural differences.

This chapter deals with some of these problems, which arise particularly when comparing annual reports from more than one country.

The amount of publication and audit varies greatly around the world. In the UK and the US there has been a long tradition of reliance on outsiders to provide finance. This led to a great deal of voluntary publication and audit, now regulated by government and professional rules. At one extreme, the UK has required publication and audit for all limited companies (nearly a million). At the other extreme, publication and audit have been rare in Switzerland and most Mediterranean countries. Even in West Germany, until the late 1980s, publication and audit were restricted to a few thousand large and public companies.

What is available?

As will be discussed in Chapter VIII, the EC Fourth Directive allows member states to exempt small companies from audit and from the publication of profit and loss accounts. Some exemptions are also allowed for medium companies. The size definitions are expressed in the Fourth Directive in European currency units (ECUs), above which member states may not go. Some examples of member state interpretations of this are shown in Table 1. A company must fall below two of the three thresholds in order to qualify.

Because there are options in the Directive and because member states can always be more severe than the Directive requires, the national laws are different. For example, the UK does not exempt small companies from audit, whereas Germany does. Although the Directive was designed to lead to a massive extension of audit for Germany, most companies are still exempted because they are 'small'; and many others are not obeying the new laws. Table 2 summarises some of the provisions for four countries.

This all implies, for example, that a German looking at a medium-sized British company should always be able to find public financial information, but that the same does not apply vice versa.

TABLE 1.	SIZE CRITERIA IN FOUR EUROPEAN COUNTRIES			
Small companies				
	UK	*France*	*Netherlands*	*Germany*
Turnover	£2 million	F 10 million	fl 8 million	DM 8 million
Balance sheet total	£0.975 million	F 5 million	fl 4 million	DM 3.9 million
Employees	50	50	50	50
Medium companies				
	UK	*France*	*Netherlands*	*Germany*
Turnover	£8 million	n/a	fl 35 million	DM 32 million
Balance sheet total	£3.9 million	n/a	fl 17 million	DM 15.5 million
Employees	250	n/a	250	250

Language

Language is very obvious as a problem for international comparisons, and it might be thought to be trivial in the sense that:

- Many people can read more than one language
- Many large companies provide translations
- Experts can always be hired to translate (and they are a lot cheaper than accountants or financiers).

TABLE 2.	EXEMPTIONS FROM PUBLICATION AND AUDIT IN FOUR EUROPEAN COUNTRIES	
Country	*Small companies*	*Medium companies*
UK	Exemption from publication (though not from audit and sending to shareholders) of profit and loss account, directors' report and many notes; and balance sheet abbreviated	Abbreviated profit and loss account (for publication purposes only)
France	Abridged accounts and notes may be published	Abridged notes in published accounts
Netherlands	Abbreviated formats for statements; also exempt from audit	Abbreviated profit and loss account
Germany	Exempt from audit	May be audited by *Vereidigte Buchprüfer* rather than by *Wirtschaftsprüfer*

TABLE 3. EXAMPLES OF US AND UK ACCOUNTING TERMINOLOGY	
US term	*UK term*
Common stock	Ordinary shares
Inventories	Stocks
Treasury stock	Own shares
Receivables	Debtors
Reserve for doubtful accounts	Provision for bad debts
Included in equity	Taken to reserves

Indeed, compared with some of the other problems mentioned above, language **is** comparatively easy. Nevertheless, there are many pitfalls to be avoided.

Starting with English, we should be aware that the accounting jargon used in the UK and the USA differs considerably. Furthermore, there is great variety within both countries, particularly in the USA. UK/US terminology is examined in some detail in the glossary to this book. The few examples in Table 3 illustrate the scope for misunderstanding.

The problem is, of course, not just that the language is different (largely because American is seventeenth-century English) but that the words exist in both languages but often mean something different. There is less scope for confusion in Japanese!

The importance of this problem is not confined to English-speaking countries. Many companies all around the world produce translations, usually into approximately American English. However, these accounts may have unreliable or misleading translations and, at worst, the English version may be little more than a marketing document. Such versions are, of course, not the real statutory accounts, nor do they have to obey UK rules, so they may be extracts or manipulations of the original.

Some examples of translation problems will help to illustrate these points. The accounts of Total Oil (for France) and AEG (for Germany) are used for this purpose. There is no suggestion that these companies are worse than any others, indeed they are better than many; it is merely that language difference is a complex problem in a technical area like accounting.

Example 1
The following is an extract from the English-language version of an annual report of Total Oil:

Foreign currency balance sheets are converted into French francs on the basis of exchange rates at 31 December 1987. The conversion is applied to fixed assets as well as to monetary assets and liabilities. Gains or losses on translation of their balance sheets at the end of the previous year are dealt with . . .

This extract shows the word 'conversion' being used interchangeably with 'translation' because the two accounting terms are the same in French (*conversion*). In English the former means a physical act of exchange, whereas the latter (which would be correct here) means an accounting manipulation.

Example 2
A further extract, as found in earlier Total Oil reports, is as follows:

However, as concerns new acquired companies the excess of the Total Group's investment in such companies . . . is capitalized in the consolidated balance sheet and is not amortized . . . These surplus values are depreciated on a straightline basis . . .

The expression 'surplus values' is a translation of *survaleurs*. The English accounting expression would have been 'goodwill'.

Example 3
The accompanying exhibit above shows one of the balance sheets of the 1988 AEG report. As may be seen, the translation is into American English, for example 'inventories' and 'trade receivables'. More interestingly, the title states 'Consolidated Balance Sheet of AEG Aktiengesellschaft'. Yet several factors prove that it is actually the parent company's **unconsolidated** balance sheet:

1. It states 'AEG Aktiengesellschaft'; that is, a company not a group.
2. If this is not the parent's balance sheet, then there is not one in the annual report, as there should be.
3. The figure for 'financial assets' is very large; it is of course the shares in the subsidiaries at cost.
4. There are no minority interests shown.

In other words, although the document states that it is consolidated, it is not. This is a form of translation problem.

CONSOLIDATED BALANCE SHEET OF AEG AKTIENGESELLSCHAFT AS OF DECEMBER 31, 1988

Assets

	Dec. 31, 1988		Dec. 31, 1987	
	Million DM	Million DM	Million DM	Million DM
Fixed and Financial Assets				
Intangible Assets	40		18	
Fixed Assets				
Cost of acquisition or production	605		329	
Accumulated depreciation	− 81		− 40	
	524		289	
Financial Assets	2,546		1,996	
		3,110		2,303
Current Assets				
Inventories				
Total	1,709		1,731	
Payments received on account	− 1,165		− 1,296	
	544		435	
Receivables and Other Assets				
Trade receivables	1,180		1,308	
Receivables from affiliated companies	669		543	
Other receivables and current assets	199		177	
	2,048		2,028	
Marketable Securities/Certificates of Indebtedness	185		367	
Cash Items	887		1,055	
		3,664		3,885
Prepaid Expenses		3		1
		6,777		6,189
Shareholders' Equity and Liabilities				
Equity				
Subscribed capital	931		931	
Capital reserves (statutory reserve)	885		885	
Revenue reserves	344		344	
Net profit	9		–	
		2,169		2,160
Accruals				
Accruals for pensions and similar obligations	1,634		1,597	
Other accruals	991		1,080	
		2,625		2,677
Financial Liabilities		257		197
Other Liabilities				
Trade payables	573		495	
Payables to affiliated companies	887		450	
Other liabilities	266		210	
		1,726		1,155
		6,777		6,189

Example 4

When matters get complicated, a translation often becomes opaque. AEG's note on consolidated techniques is very difficult to understand. It is shown below with the present author's interpretation. The technical points are discussed further in Chapter V.

Original	*Author's interpretation*
Capital consolidation is performed using the 'book value method'. Under this method, the book values of the affiliated companies are netted against the underlying equity in these companies at the time of acquisition or initial consolidation.	Full consolidation is performed using a version of fair value accounting. Under this method, the first stage is to compare the cost of the consolidated companies with the book value of the group's share of their net assets. Generally this is done at the date of acquisition, but for existing subsidiaries that have been consolidated for the first time this year, the year-end values are used.
Where the book values exceed underlying equity, the difference is allocated to the respective assets or liabilities according to their real value. A difference remaining after the allocation is shown as goodwill or disclosed as a reduction from the reserves.	Where cost exceeds net assets, the difference is allocated to the subsidiary's assets and liabilities up to and in proportion to their fair values. Any excess remaining is goodwill, which is either shown as an asset or written off against reserves.
If the book values fall below the underlying equity, the difference is recorded as 'reserve arising from consolidation'.	Where the initial exercise leads to a negative difference, this is shown as a 'reserve arising from consolidation'.

The general problem illustrated by these examples is that, although the language may be of good quality, the translation is often not done by accountants, perhaps because bilingual accountants are very expensive to hire. For example, there are no such terms in British accounting as 'surplus values' (Example 2) or 'capital consolidation' and 'book value method' (Example 4). Of course, none of this should be read as implying a lack of gratitude for translations: it is a very rare US or UK company that bothers at all.

In order to help the reader as far as possible in cases where there is no translation, there is a six-language glossary of terms at the end of this book. An Anglo-American comparison and a detailed explanation of terms can also be found in the glossary.

It is often cheaper for the company than the report readers to do some-thing about the problems of interpreting international differences. Com-panies wishing to raise money on the international markets may volun-teer, or may be forced in the case of some stock exchange rules, to help the readers in one or more of the following ways:

What multi-nationals do to help

- Where possible, choose accounting policies for statutory domestic purposes that are most in line with international practices. For example, some Swiss companies volunteer to consolidate or to capitalise leases. At the extreme, Royal Dutch/Shell tries to comply with US, UK and Dutch rules simultaneously. Companies may also volunteer for an Anglo-American audit when this is not legally necessary.
- Provide versions of the annual report which translate only the language, and which may raise the problems discussed above. This is common for European companies into English.
- Provide reports in another currency. For example, some Japanese companies (such as Fujitsu, NTT) provide dollar and yen figures (see Chapter VII); the International Thomson organisation provides accounts in sterling although it is of Canadian registration. These are sometimes called 'convenience statements', and the year-end translation rate is normally applied to all items.
- Provide reconciliation statements of net income or net assets from the company's domestic rules to another set. This is most obviously found in the case of companies obeying some SEC rules, when a reconcilia-tion to US GAAP is shown as a supplementary statement (e.g. Volvo, see Chapter IV; and British Airways, see Chapter II).
- Carry out 'limited restatement' of some accounting policies or formats of presentation, presumably as a supplement to domestic reports. This is quite normal for Japanese companies towards US practices.
- Publish a substantial reworking and retranslation of the annual report into another set of practices and terms (e.g. Philips). This amounts to the provision of secondary financial statements.

It is not just accounting terms and accounting practices that must be disentangled before successful international comparison. There are also different social, cultural and economic backgrounds. Let us take two examples.

Non-accounting differences

German loans

Because of the long history of debt finance in Germany, it is normal for

German companies to have a high gearing ratio compared with US or UK firms. However, not only is this traditional, it is also safer in Germany because of the long-run nature of bank interests in German industry. Bankers would be expected to pump money **into** an ailing company rather than to try to be the first to 'pull the plug'.

So a high gearing ratio is more normal and less dangerous in Germany. We will see later that accounting differences probably make German ratios look higher as well.

British, French and Italian pensions

Table 4 shows how the accounting treatment of supplementary employee remuneration influences the computation of the interesting total 'funds generated from operations' for three companies – one British, one Italian and one French.

We start with the British company, which places all pension provisions with a financial institution so that the 'funds' in question leave the company. Next, for the company operating in France, there is a statutory requirement that part of the company's profits be allocated for the benefit

---

TABLE 4. THE IMPACT OF DIFFERENT REMUNERATION SCHEMES ON FUNDS GENERATED FROM OPERATIONS

	UK (£)	France (F)	Italy (L)
Earnings	100	1,000	100,000
Add back:			
Depreciation of fixed assets	250	2,500	250,000
Provision for employee pensions	80	–	–
less Funds applied in the current year	(80)	–	–
Share of profits attributable to employees	–	800	–
less Funds applied in the current year	–	(700)	–
Deferred employee remuneration	–	–	80,000
less Funds applied in the current year	–	–	(30,000)
Funds generated from operations	350	3,600	400,000

Source: S.J. McLeay, Chapter 7 of C.W. Nobes and R.H. Parker, *Issues in Multinational Accounting*, Philip Allan, 1988.

of employees, with reinvestment in external assets within two years. In the short term, we could consider that there is an element in 'funds generated from operations' (+ F 800 in the example) which relates to the allocation for the current period, whilst the only outflow is the cash placed in external investments (− F 700).

Now compare these two approaches with the situation in Italy, where employees are entitled on leaving a company to one month's salary (at current rates of pay) for each year in service. There is no requirement for the company to place these funds in earmarked investments, although the appropriate provisions must be made. Thus, 'funds generated from operations' includes the provision (+ L 80,000) net of the payment to retiring employees (− L 30,000).

Of course, there are many ways of constructing a funds statement, and the example is not uncontentious. However, it does show that, when we compare the funds generated by companies in different countries, part of the explanation of the variability in levels of self-financing lies in the different social systems within which the companies operate.

II. ANGLO-AMERICAN ACCOUNTING

Why start here?

Now that it is clear that there are great variations in financial reporting practices, a major problem with international analysis is to decide which benchmark to use for comparisons of companies. In this book, an Anglo-American benchmark is chosen. This is partly because of the great number of listed companies in the US and UK (see Chapter III), and partly because worldwide accounting and its interpretation are so heavily influenced by Anglo-American companies, accountancy firms and financial intermediaries.

Nevertheless, it is vital to realise that there is great variety of practice **within** the UK and **within** the US, and that there are great differences **between** the UK and the US. This chapter investigates these differences. The intention is to establish an Anglo-American basis so that other countries can be examined from this. Later in the book (Chapter IX) a more precise benchmark, based on a particular version of Anglo-American practices, will be proposed.

Why are UK and US practices different?

In the next chapter, the background to worldwide differences is examined. We will look at legal systems, tax systems, corporate finance and so on. However, most of these factors do not help to explain why the UK and US should be different, because these two countries share the following:

- English common law system, which encourages private professional regulation of accounting
- Long history of widespread ownership of shares and developed stock exchanges, with consequent pressure for published financial reports and external auditors
- Separation of financial accounting from tax accounting, enabling a 'fair view' to be the paramount objective of annual reports
- Strong and large accountancy professions that can develop accounting rules and persuade companies to adopt them
- Anglo-American accountancy firms with great influence over accounting and auditing
- Lack of importance of theory; accounting is seen as a practical subject.

It seems then that an explanation is needed **not** for why US and UK accounting might be different, but for why they are not the **same**. Indeed, the problem is worse than that. In the mid nineteenth century, US financial reporting and auditing were not highly developed; they were subsequently heavily influenced by British practice. The influence came very directly in the export of British accountants to the United States, largely in order to check up on British investments.

Some of the names of those who took British accounting to the US are still well known. Arthur Young left Glasgow to set up a practice in Chicago. James Marwick and Roger Mitchell went from Glasgow to New York. Arthur Andersen was not Scottish (as the spelling of his name confirms) but he was articled to the originally British firm of Price Waterhouse, one of whose early US senior partners was George O. May (who had been articled to a firm of accountants in Exeter). So the story goes on.

British accounting arrived in the US in a familiar legal and institutional setting, and it is not surprising that many transatlantic similarities survive. Therefore, it may be necessary to resort to 'accidents' to explain the differences. For example, the economic crisis in the US in the late 1920s and early 1930s produced the Securities and Exchange Acts, which diverted US accounting from its previous course by introducing extensive SEC disclosure requirements and control (usually by threat only) of accounting standards. For its part, the UK has enacted uniform formats and many other detailed accounting rules for published accounts as a result of the EC Fourth Directive, which was based on the 1965 West German Aktiengesetz. The UK did not join the EC in order to change its accounting, but this has happened 'by accident'.

In the next section, there is an examination of the important institutions that control US and UK accounting. Then the detailed differences between US and UK accounting are analysed. However, this chapter suggests that many of these differences, although important in terms of millions of dollars, may not be based on major underlying distinctions and may prove to be short-lived.

Chapter I looked at language differences, including those between English and 'American' English, and Chapter IV looks at presentational differences between the UK, the US and other countries.

Where the rules come from

The rules that control financial reporting and auditing in the US come from three main sources: the Securities and Exchange Commission (SEC), the Financial Accounting Standards Board (FASB), and the American Institute of Certified Public Accountants (AICPA). In the UK, the rules come from Companies Acts and from the accounting standards of the Accounting Standards Board.

The context of accounting and auditing in the US is different from that in many other developed countries in that there are no generalised legal requirements relating to most or all companies. By contrast, the UK is a fairly extreme case, because company law requires **all** companies, however small, to draw up full accounts for shareholders, to have them independently audited, and to make them public (in some cases in abbreviated form).

In the US, there are state laws relating to the incorporation of companies and their subsequent behaviour. However, audit and publication of accounts are not generally required of companies. Federal law only becomes important for those companies that wish to create a market in their securities. Such companies must register with the government regulatory agency, the Securities and Exchange Commission, and then obey its rules.

The analogous action in most other developed countries would be to form a 'public company' – a form of legal entity which is allowed to create a market in its securities. There is no direct US equivalent to 'public' and 'private' companies, partly because this is a new-fangled distinction in Britain, introduced well after 1776! Instead, there are just 'companies' which register with the appropriate state authorities by depositing their bylaws and certificate of incorporation (equivalent to the memorandum and articles of association in the UK).

The US Securities and Exchange Commission

The SEC is headed by a five-member board appointed by the President of the USA. It was set up under the Securities Acts of 1933 and 1934, which govern new issues and the exchange of securities. The SEC also has power over the financial reporting and audit of companies registered with it. In more detail, registration becomes necessary if a company wishes to be listed on a major market such as the New York Stock Exchange or the American Stock Exchange (also in New York City), or if it wishes its shares to be traded on an unlisted securities market or (above a certain size) to be traded over the counter. Also, for example, a British company that wished to acquire an intended US subsidiary by buying out its American shareholders partly or wholly with British parent company shares would have to be registered with the SEC because it would be offering its shares to US citizens. Something like 11,000 companies fit into these various categories.

When a company registers with the SEC, a large number of responsibilities descend upon it. First, the SEC requires preparation and filing of annual financial statements. The SEC checks receipt of the statements, which is a condition of continued registration. The filed accounts then become matters of public record, and may be consulted by anyone via the SEC. In this sense, the SEC is analogous to the British Registry of Companies or to continental commercial registries. However, the SEC has comparatively few companies to monitor, and is able to carry out its task in a more detailed way than registries in other countries.

The second SEC requirement is for audit of the annual financial statements by an independent certified public accountant (CPA). As with publication, this would be a generalised legal requirement in other countries, but government-backed compulsion applies only to SEC-registered companies in the US.

The third point is that certain forms must be filled in and filed. For example, Form 10-K must be prepared annually. This is a document whose contents somewhat resemble a directors' report in the UK. It contains, for example, information on:

- Remuneration and shareholdings of directors and officers
- Principal shareholdings
- Number of equity shareholders
- Interests of management in certain transactions.

In addition there is a requirement to report quarterly (on Form 10-Q) on such details as sales and income. This is unaudited information which is analogous to the interim reporting required by the International Stock Exchange in London. However, the SEC's requirement is **quarterly** and covers more companies than those listed on any particular exchange. There is also a requirement to report 'unusual' events, such as a change of auditors or the issue of more shares. These events would be expected to be of interest to shareholders and others, so the SEC requires them to be made public in a standard way.

The fourth type of SEC instruction relates to the content and appearance of the annual financial statements. These are to some extent governed by SEC rules, such as Regulation S-X or Regulation S-K. For example, Article 11A of Regulation S-X calls for the publication of statements of cash flows. Regulation S-K contains many requirements concerning note disclosures. The Regulations also require **three** years' figures in income statements and cash flow statements, compared with one or two (this year and last year) in most other countries.

The fifth requirement is that registrants should use 'generally accepted accounting principles' (GAAP) in their filed financial statements. The next sections of this chapter examine the content of GAAP in detail. At this point, it should be said that the SEC normally allows others to determine GAAP, although sometimes it does intervene through documents called Financial Reporting Releases (formerly Accounting Series Releases). It is interesting to note that, although the existence of a government agency like the SEC seems a rather un-American piece of interference, in practice the agency leaves the detail to professionals, as one would expect in a country with an English legal system. A French or German SEC would ensure that any rules were made by government bodies, not by private clubs!

Voluntary publication and audit in the US

In summary, all the important rules for financial reporting and auditing are required and monitored by the SEC, if not actually set by them. So the difference between the requirements for SEC-registered companies and for others is very great – much larger than the differences between British listed public, unlisted public and private companies. Having said that, many US corporations 'volunteer' to follow GAAP or to have CPA auditors. The reasons for this are many, but include:

- Preparation for becoming SEC registered
- Requirements imposed by shareholders or by articles of association (bylaws) of the company
- Requirements in loan stock agreements
- Requirements imposed by banks or other lenders.

In addition, although the subsidiaries of SEC registrants do not have to publish audited financial statements, their accounts are included in the consolidated financial statements of the SEC-registered group. Thus, by implication, the activities of the subsidiaries come within the scope of GAAP and audit.

British laws

There is no UK equivalent of the SEC. Instead there are Companies Acts which relate to all companies. These Acts stretch back to 1844. They regulate the formation and management of companies; the compulsory publication of annual accounts and audit; the contents of accounts; insolvency; and many other matters. However, as in the US, the detail of accounting rules is still largely in standards.

US and UK Accounting Standards

In the US, the professionally set rules that contribute to 'generally accepted accounting principles' (GAAP) include:

- ARBs: Accounting Research Bulletins of the AICPA's former Committee on Accounting Procedure
- APB Opinions: issued by the AICPA's former Accounting Principles Board
- SFASs: Statements of Financial Accounting Standards of the FASB.

The FASB is an independent body which has issued over 100 standards since its foundation in 1973. Very occasionally the SEC overrules the FASB, but usually SFASs amount to law for SEC-registered companies.

In the UK in 1990 the former professional Accounting Standards Committee (ASC) was replaced by an independent body with greater resources and power. The new body, the Accounting Standards Board, has taken over the existing standards of the ASC. The UK standards are less numerous, less detailed and less enforceable than US standards, but they do apply to all companies because all companies have to publish audited 'true and fair' reports. UK principles are embodied in Statements of Standard Accounting Practice (SSAPs).

The reader may be wondering what there is left for the AICPA and the UK professional bodies to do, since they have given up control of standard setting. Several functions remain. First, they are concerned with the regulations governing entry to the profession. In addition, they control the codes of professional ethics. They are also the guardians of what in the US are called 'generally accepted auditing standards' (GAAS), which consist of the Statements on Auditing Standards published by the Auditing Standards Board of the AICPA and the Auditing Practices Committee in the UK.

Audit

The audit report of an SEC-registered corporation will contain references to the following elements:

- Prepared by CPA
- CPA has used GAAS
- Company has used GAAP
- GAAP have been consistently used (given that choices are available even within GAAP)
- Financial statements '**present fairly** in accordance with GAAP'.

It has already been mentioned that only about 11,000 US corporations have SEC-imposed audits by CPAs. As a result the following may occur for non-registrants:

Voluntary full CPA audit   This may be undertaken because of debt covenants or bylaw requirements. The work done by the auditor and the rules used in the preparation of the financial statements will be the same as those above. The audit report will contain the five elements mentioned above.

Audit review by a CPA   'Audit review' is a technical term, and refers to work done in accordance with a specific set of AICPA rules. The audit review will not be in accordance with full GAAP or full GAAS, but it will probably be enough to satisfy the Internal Revenue Service and the average banker.

Compilation   Such a service may also be performed by a CPA. It involves the preparation of financial statements from the records (sometimes incomplete) of the business. However, no audit checks will directly have been performed.

In the UK, all companies must be fully audited by qualified auditors. They check that the accounts comply with company law and give a true and fair view. The latter normally implies conformity with standards.

In conclusion, many sets of US corporate financial statements may involve work by CPAs but yet not be fully audited. It is necessary to be much more careful in the US than in the UK about what exactly has been done. Worse, since most corporations do not require an audit at all, let alone an audit by CPAs, a company may present financial statements 'audited' by those who are not professionally qualified. The less expert and reliable the 'auditors', the more are they likely to copy elements of the full audit report discussed above. So, it will be worth checking whether the auditors are CPAs.

Asset valuation   Property, plant and equipment

The basic valuation rule in the US (and Canada) is that property, plant and equipment ('fixed assets' in UK terminology) must be valued at historical cost, and depreciated where appropriate. This aspect of GAAP is an early requirement of the SEC and is a response to unbridled upward revaluations in the 1920s as some US corporations tried to disguise the worsening financial situation.

Many large UK companies do show fixed assets, particularly land and buildings, at a valuation above historical cost. Indeed, in the UK, investment properties (generally, those that are not owner occupied) must be revalued annually at market values and must not be depreciated, according to SSAP 19.

As a result, comparisons of US and UK financial statements would need to bear this major difference in mind. The effect on 'total assets' or 'net assets' or 'equity' (and therefore on ratios involving these aggregates) can be enormous.

Inventory valuation
The almost universal rule of 'the lower of cost and market' is used in the US. However, 'market' tends to mean replacement cost in the US, whereas it means net realisable value in the UK.

The major feature of US inventory valuation is that the majority of companies use the last in, first out (LIFO) method of determining the cost of inventory. This is one of the largest differences in terms of millions of dollars between US and UK accounting. There is no particular international difference of theory that explains this difference in practice; it is merely that LIFO is allowed for inventory valuation for the purposes of taxation in the US but not in most other countries. For example, LIFO is not acceptable for tax purposes in the UK; it is also largely unavailable for accounting purposes, because SSAP 9 makes it clear that LIFO will not normally give a fair view of closing inventory.

The use of LIFO means that the most recently purchased inventory is deemed to be the earliest used up in production of sales, leaving the oldest inventory to be included in the closing inventory at the year end. When the price of a particular type of inventory is rising, this means that income is lower and the closing inventory is also lower than it would be when using the alternative methods of average cost or first in, first out (FIFO).

LIFO is allowed for tax purposes in the US in order that it may act as a relief from the taxation of inventory-holding gains during periods of inflation. Otherwise, tax would have to be paid on income that is tied up in the extra value (though not volume) of inventory. The problem for US accounting is that the tax rules require companies to use LIFO for the published income statements if it is used for tax purposes. This is reminiscent of the effect of tax rules on continental European accounting, except that it is all-pervasive there. The British equivalent of LIFO for tax purposes was stock appreciation relief, which operated from 1973 to 1984. However, this relief did not affect the UK rules for financial reporting.

The majority of US companies take advantage of the tax reductions made possible by the use of LIFO. However, as Table 5 shows, most companies actually use a mixture of methods, presumably because some inventories fall in price. Those companies still using FIFO may be doing so in order to keep profits up, perhaps because management compensation is linked to declared net income. The rule requiring consistent ap-

---

TABLE 5. COST DETERMINATION FOR INVENTORY VALUATION BY 600 LARGE US COMPANIES (A COMPANY MAY USE MORE THAN ONE METHOD)

Inventory methods: instances of use

LIFO	393
FIFO	383
Average cost	223
Other	53
	1,052

Use of LIFO: number of companies

For all inventories	23
For 50% or more	229
For less than 50%	74
Not determinable	67
	393

TABLE 6.	THE EFFECTS OF LIFO ON INVENTORY ($ MILLION)			
	LIFO	Adjustment	FIFO	% adjustment
General Electric, 1987	6,265	+ 2,076	8,341	+ 33
General Motors, 1988	7,984	+ 2,525	10,509	+ 32
Caterpillar, 1986	1,211	+ 1,634	2,845	+ 135
Goodyear, 1986	1,352	+ 290	1,642	+ 21

plication of GAAP ought to stop frequent changes from LIFO to FIFO and back.

The effects of the use of LIFO can be very great. As far as the valuation of closing inventory is concerned, the prices involved can be not just slightly out of date but **decades** old. That is, LIFO retains costs of inventory from whenever that type of inventory was first bought. Thus, closing inventory valuations may be very unrealistically low. This might be seen to be more serious than out-of-date fixed asset valuation because inventory is nearer to being sold and it forms a major element in liquidity ratios. Even worse, when inventories are physically reduced, perhaps because production shifts to the use of a more modern material, very old costs of inventory may pass through the income statement. This might be called 'eating into old LIFO layers of inventory'. This would lead to misleading income statements, although it might be claimed that LIFO normally gives a better picture of income because cost of sales includes more current costs.

GAAP requires companies to disclose which method of inventory valuation is being used, and the SEC requires its registrant companies that use LIFO to disclose in the notes what the value of inventory would be using FIFO.

Table 6 summarises the effects of using LIFO as disclosed in the notes to four financial statements. The largest proportional effect is in the case of Caterpillar, where use of FIFO would have resulted in the following adjustments to accounting numbers and ratios:

- Inventory: increase by 135%
- Current assets: increase by 49%
- Net current assets: increase by 138%
- Net assets: increase by 52%
- Shareholders' funds: increase by 52%
- Current ratio: increase from 1.54 to 2.29.

Of course, the above figures represent the cumulative effect of using LIFO. There is also an effect each year on the calculation of income, usually a negative one.

If an overseas reader of US financial statements made no other adjust-ment in order to enhance international comparison, the relatively simple adjustment for LIFO would be a major step forward.

Research and development

The relevant US GAAP for R&D is to be found in SFAS 2, which requires all expenditures on R&D to be treated as expense immediately, unless of course they create physical fixed assets such as a laboratory. This is more conservative than the UK standard, which allows certain development oxponditurco to bc capitalised; that is, carried forward as assets in order to be matched against future related revenues. This is explained in SSAP 13.

There is no substantial difference in theory between SFAS 2 and SSAP 13. They both discuss the conflict between prudence (expense at once) and accruals (carry forward for matching). However, SFAS 2 concludes that, on balance, prudence and a desire for uniformity call for a straight-forward prohibition on capitalisation.

There is also little transatlantic difference in practices, because most British companies choose not to capitalise development expenditures even though they could. This means that international comparisons are only made difficult for those few British companies for whom development expenditure is very important and is capitalised; for example, in the aerospace industry. Fortunately, both SFAS 2 and SSAP 13 (as revised in 1988) require note disclosure of the annual R&D expense.

A specific exception to the US prohibition on capitalisation concerns computer software products. SFAS 86 allows the costs of developing such products to be capitalised under certain conditions when the technical feasibility of the product has been established. Thereafter, the capitalised costs must be shown at the lower of unamortised cost and net realisable value.

Capitalisation of leases

The idea of capitalising leases is an American invention. It is designed to achieve the dominance of 'substance over form'. That is, in order to present fairly the assets and liabilities of a company with leased assets, it is necessary to present the economic substance of the leasing trans-actions rather than their legal form. In the case of many leases, the lessee expects to have use of the leased assets for most of their useful lives and to make a series of payments to the lessor which amount to approximately the original fair value of the assets. That is, the leasing transaction is very similar to a loan followed by a purchase of the assets.

The basic US rules for lease accounting are to be found in SFAS 13, on which the UK rules in SSAP 21 are loosely based. Not all leases fall to be capitalised. For example, a three-month lease of a car would be excluded. SFAS 13 establishes the following criteria, any **one** of which implies capitalisation:

1. By the end of the lease term, ownership is transferred to the lessee.
2. There is a bargain-purchase option during or at the end of the lease term; this would amount to the transfer of ownership.
3. The term of the lease is 75% or more of the useful life of the asset.
4. At the start of the lease, the present value of the minimum lease payments is 90% or more of the fair value of the asset.

It was noted earlier that US accounting rules tend to look like laws. This precise codification of the nature of 'finance' or 'capital' leases is a good example of that process. It appears to encourage those who wish to avoid capitalising the asset and the liability to try to arrange lease contracts where, for example, the term of the lease is 74% of the useful life of the asset. By contrast, the UK criterion for capitalisation in SSAP 21 is based on the last item above and is expressed in a 'spirit' rather than 'letter' of the law way. SSAP 21 requires a lease to be capitalised if it transfers substantially all the risks and rewards of ownership to the lessee. This is presumed to occur when the present value of the minimum lease payments amounts to '**substantially** all (**normally** 90% or more) of the fair value of the leased asset' (emphases added). Hire purchase contracts (corresponding to bargain-purchase leases) are also capitalised in the UK.

When a lease is capitalised, an asset and a lease liability are accounted for equal to the lesser of the fair value of the asset (i.e. what it could have been bought for at arm's length at the inception of the lease) and the present value of the minimum lease payments. SSAP 21 gives a hint that the fair value of the asset will normally be appropriate.

Depreciation of the capitalised asset is clearly necessary, as a charge for using it up and as a provision to reduce its carrying value in the balance sheet. Under the US rules, the length of depreciable life depends on which of the above four criteria for classification was relevant. For reasons 1 and 2, the life is the physical life of the asset; for reasons 3 and 4, it is the lease life. As usual, the UK rule is simpler: the life is the lesser of the physical and lease lives.

The most complex part of lease accounting is splitting up the annual payments to the lessor into two parts: the finance charge and the reduction in the capitalised lease liability. The aim is to equalise the annual finance charges in relation to the outstanding liabilities at any time.

The face of US or UK balance sheets will not normally show capitalised leases separately, but the details will be found in notes.

Interest capitalisation

For many years it has been the practice of some US companies to include in the 'cost' of certain self-constructed properties the capitalised interest on loans that had been taken out to construct them. This applies when the assets have an 'acquisition period' during which they are prepared for their intended use (either sale or internal use). Loans do not have to be specifically designated for any particular project, but the capitalising company must make actual payments of interest to a lender before interest can be capitalised. The amounts capitalised in any period must be disclosed.

UK practice varies, although the Companies Act 1985 allows capitalisation. Some construction companies do capitalise interest, though disclosure is generally poor.

The topics in the previous section obviously affect income, given that costs which are not capitalised will be expenses, and vice versa. This section deals with some other matters that are obviously and directly related to income. In both the UK and the US, the general principles of conservatism (prudence), consistency and matching (accruals) apply.

Income measurement

Deferred tax

The major point here, in terms of millions of dollars, is that US companies are required to account fully for deferred tax whereas there is only partial accounting for it in the UK. However, this discussion should begin with an explanation of the causes of deferred tax.

Deferred tax is caused by reversible timing differences between the treatment of an item as a revenue or expense for accounting purposes and its treatment for tax purposes. For example, for tax purposes, companies may be allowed to charge depreciation (capital allowances in the UK) at a faster rate than that based on estimates of the lives and scrap values of the assets concerned. The latter rate will be used by companies to establish the charge for depreciation for accounting purposes. Thus, tax depreciation will be larger than accounting depreciation in the early years of an asset's life. However, this will reverse in the later years. In a sense, then, the tax liabilities are artificially low in the early years. Accounting for deferred tax tries to correct for this. This is an example of the convention of accruals or matching, which attempts to ensure that expenses fall in the periods to which they relate, irrespective of cash payment dates.

The technique for achieving full accounting for deferred tax is to increase (debit) the tax for the year in the income statement to what it would have been without the generous tax rules. The counter-balancing effect is to create a deferred tax account (credit), which one could interpret

TABLE 7. CAUSES OF TIMING DIFFERENCES RESULTING IN DEFERRED TAX IN 600 LARGE US COMPANIES

Depreciation	488
Pensions	110
Other employee benefits	112
Discontinued operations	98
Instalment sales	88
Inventory valuation	86
Unremitted earnings	70
Long-term contracts	67
Interest and taxes during construction	51
Leases	27
Intangible drilling costs	26
Warranties	16

as a liability to pay more tax in the future. Both accounting entries may seem unattractive to management: the debit makes earnings look lower; the credit makes liabilities look worse.

Table 7 shows, for 600 large US corporations, the major causes of timing differences that gave rise to deferred tax accounting. The major cause in the UK is also depreciation timing differences.

UK out of line
By the mid 1970s, there was a consensus in the English-speaking world (and The Netherlands) that companies should fully account for deferred tax. The rules were to be found in APB Opinion 11 in the US, and SSAP 11 in the UK. However, for various reasons, deferred tax entries were especially large in the UK. As a result, deferred tax balances became amongst the largest items in the balance sheet of many UK companies. Because deferred tax accounting has unattractive effects on financial statements, company directors began to complain loudly that the balances were misleading because they were not expected to be **paid**. This is because, assuming normal continuation of the business and of inflation, reversing timing differences would always at least be balanced by new timing differences in any year. So, corporation tax was continually postponed, and therefore was never expected to be paid, and therefore was not a liability, and therefore should not be accounted for.

This strong pressure led to a revision of UK rules by the issue of SSAP 15 to replace SSAP 11 in 1978. SSAP 15 calls for partial accounting for deferred tax, that is accounting for it only when the tax is actually expected to be paid in the foreseeable future, which is not usual for most timing differences. It should be noted that the UK view represents a concentration on the balance sheet (is there a liability?), whereas the original US view stressed the income statement (what is the correctly matched tax expense for the year?).

A further detailed difference follows from this. The US approach of APB Opinion 11 ignored changes in corporate income tax rates, because they did not affect the year for which the deferred tax accounting had been done. By contrast, since SSAP 15 concentrates on the existence of a real liability, any change in corporation tax **does** affect the expected liability. To be exact, the relevant rate is the one that **will be** ruling when the liability is eventually settled. However, that of course is a guess, so accountants normally use the present rate as the best estimate of the future rate. The APB method is called the 'deferral method', and that of SSAP 15 the 'liability method'.

New US method

This logic of choice of the US deferral and the UK liability methods was confused in 1988 by the release of SFAS 96 by the FASB. After many years of accumulating deferred tax credits, these numbers have become embarrassingly large in the US as they had earlier done in the UK. The US response was **not** to move to partial accounting for deferred tax (as in SSAP 15), but to amend APB Opinion 11 by requiring changes in corporate income tax rates to be taken into account. To be cynical, this decision looked as though it was due to the substantial fall in tax rates in 1987 which greatly reduced the deferred tax credit balances under the SFAS 96 method. The introduction of SFAS 96 was delayed several times, but it will mean that US companies will use the liability method even though the reason that they are accounting for deferred tax is not that they expect to pay it.

The effect of these differences on transatlantic comparisons can be very large. For example, deferred tax credits and their proportion of shareholders' funds were, for General Motors in 1987, $2,145 million and 6.5%; and for Goodyear in 1986, $586 million and 19.5%.

Extraordinary items

The general concept of extraordinary items is similar on both sides of the Atlantic, although in some continental European countries the concept is either much broader or does not exist at all. For US and UK companies, extraordinary items are generally distinguished as being material, infrequent and unusual for the business. Further, in both countries, extraordinary items are shown separately from others, are shown net of tax and are excluded from operating earnings.

However, there are some differences. First, 'infrequent' is more tightly defined in the US as 'not reasonably expected to recur in the foreseeable future'. Secondly, in the UK gains or losses on major restructuring may be treated as extraordinary, and the same applies to gains and losses on the sale of discontinued businesses. In the US, these are generally not treated as extraordinary. On the other hand, the US rules (but not those of the UK) always require gains or losses on early retirements of debt to be treated as extraordinary, even if they are frequent and usual.

Disclosures

As a point on disclosure, US GAAP (but not UK practice) requires income from subsequently discontinued operations to be disclosed separately in the income statement. In both countries one would also expect to see disclosure in the notes of unusual (in the UK, exceptional) items that might recur but are abnormal in size or incidence.

The main US rules in this area can be found in APB Opinions 9 and 30, and in SFAS 4. In the UK, the rules are in SSAP 6, which also covers prior-period adjustments, restricting them to the correction of fundamental errors of the past and to changes in accounting policies. In the US, prior-period adjustments are restricted still further (by APB Opinions 9 and 20, and SFAS 16) to corrections of errors and to certain adjustments to tax losses on acquisition of a subsidiary.

Dividends

There is a major difference of practice under this heading, owing to the fact that dividends in the US are not regarded as being related to a particular period of a company's activities. Consequently, US practice is to account for a dividend only when it is formally declared. It is then treated as a deduction from equity, and an increase in a current liability (settled on payment to the stockholders). This contrasts with the UK treatment of linking dividends to a particular year's profit, and therefore making a provision at a year end for the dividend that will be subsequently recommended by the directors and approved at an annual general meeting. The effect of this is generally that, at a year end, one extra year's worth of dividends has been deducted from shareholders' equity in the case of UK companies.

Pension costs

The main US rules on this complex subject are to be found in SFAS 87, and those of the UK in SSAP 24. Given the great variety that would be **possible** for pension cost accounting, the two standards are fairly similar. As usual, the US rules preceded the UK rules and they are more detailed; for example, SFAS 87 specifies actuarial methods and assumptions and it requires more disclosures than SSAP 24 does.

The basis for the charge is also different. In the UK the charge against profit is based on the amount paid to the pension scheme; the funding requirements drive the accounting charge. In the US, the charge is made up of:

> **Service cost**, which is the actuarial cost of benefits accruing in the period
>
> *plus* **Interest cost**, which is designed to finance the liabilities relating to all past service
>
> *less* **Estimated return on assets**, which is the return on invested assets that might approximately cover the interest cost.

There will have to be adjustments for changing estimates or benefits.

Consolidation

International differences in consolidation practices are so important for interpretation of accounts that a whole chapter is devoted to them (Chapter V). Consolidation is largely an American invention, so the USA features prominently in that chapter.

In order to concentrate here on the US/UK differences, the most obvious area of concern is goodwill accounting, in particular the treatment of goodwill once it has been calculated. The long-established US practice has been to treat goodwill as an asset, and gradually to amortise it against income over a period of up to 40 years. This is required by APB Opinion 17.

The UK treatment for most companies has been to deduct goodwill immediately from reserves. So, it is never shown as an asset and never charged against profit. This means that US group statements will tend to show higher net assets but lower income.

In 1990 the ASC, in its last few months of life, issued a proposal (ED 47) to follow the US route approximately. This was heavily opposed by companies.

Recap

Although US and UK accounting are similar in a world context, this chapter has shown that there are many important differences. For example:

Jargon There are many differences in technical terms (see Chapter I and the glossary).

Publication and audit UK rules require **all** companies to publish audited financial statements. The US rules are more strongly enforced but apply only to the 11,000 or so SEC-registered companies and to those others that 'volunteer' for commercial or contract reasons.

Formats US balance sheets are generally based on the horizontal version; current assets precede fixed assets; and there is considerable variation. UK balance sheets are now more standardised: they are nearly always vertical, starting with fixed assets (see Chapter IV).

Fixed assets   US GAAP requires fixed assets to be valued at historical cost (depreciated where appropriate). The practice of many large UK companies is very different from this, involving occasional or annual revaluations to a current value.

Inventory   Most US corporations use LIFO for at least some of their inventories. This usually reduces income and inventory values, sometimes drastically. It is not a generally accepted practice in the UK.

Deferred tax   US practice is to account fully for deferred tax, using the liability method from the late 1980s. UK practice is partially to account for deferred tax (i.e. only when an actual liability is foreseen); the liability method is used.

Goodwill   Goodwill is capitalised and amortised through the income statement in the US. In the UK, goodwill is nearly always written immediately against reserves, with no asset shown and no charge against income.

A further way of summarising the differences is to examine a Form 20-F, the document which foreign registrants must provide for the SEC if they do not produce full US GAAP annual reports. Form 20-F illustrates the adjustments that would be necessary to move to US GAAP; the example below is for British Airways.

EXTRACT 1.   FROM THE ANNUAL REPORT OF BRITISH AIRWAYS PLC FOR 1987–88

UNITED STATES GENERALLY ACCEPTED ACCOUNTING PRINCIPLES (US GAAP) INFORMATION

The financial statements are prepared in accordance with accounting principles generally accepted in the United Kingdom which differ in certain respects from those generally accepted in the United States. The significant differences are described below.

(i) Deferred taxation

BA provides for deferred taxation on the liability method on all material timing differences to the extent that it is probable that the liabilities will crystallise. Under US GAAP, as set out in Statement of Financial Accounting Standards 96 (FAS 96), deferred taxation is generally provided on a full liability basis. For the purposes of the reconciliation below, the cumulative effect on prior years resulting from the change in the method of accounting for deferred taxation from the deferral method, as required by FAS 96, has been reflected as a change in accounting principle in the year ended 31 March 1988.

(ii) Goodwill

BA writes off goodwill arising on consolidation directly against retained earnings. Under US GAAP, goodwill arising on consolidation is amortised over its useful life. For the purposes of determining the differences between UK GAAP and US GAAP, the expected useful life of goodwill has been taken to be forty years.

(iii) Property and fleet valuation

Under US GAAP tangible assets must be stated at cost less accumulated depreciation in the financial statements. The valuation of properties incorporated by BA in its financial statements in the year ended 31 March 1984 and the valuation of fleet incorporated at 31 March 1988, would not therefore have been included in financial statements prepared in accordance with US GAAP and, in the case of properties, subsequent charges for depreciation would have been correspondingly lower. When such assets are sold, however, any surplus arising would be reflected in income.

(iv) Purchase accounting

Under US GAAP, as set out in FAS 96, a deferred tax liability is recognised for the tax effects of differences between the assigned fair values and tax bases of assets acquired, whereas under UK GAAP no such liability is recognised. As a result of recognising such a deferred tax liability the amount of goodwill arising on consolidation increases correspondingly. Under US GAAP the deferred tax liability would be amortised over the same period as the assets to which it relates.

(v) Forward exchange contracts

Under US GAAP the notional gain or loss on foreign currency forward exchange contracts, arising on the translation of outstanding contracts at each balance sheet date at the rates of exchange ruling at that date, would have been included in the determination of net income. BA does not take account of such notional gains and losses.

(vi) Dividends

Under US GAAP dividends are only incorporated in financial statements when declared. The proposed final dividend, and related advance Corporation Tax, would not therefore have been included in financial statements prepared in accordance with US GAAP.

(vii) Extraordinary items

Under US GAAP the amounts reported as extraordinary items would not have been deemed to be extraordinary items and would have been included in the determination of income before extraordinary items with no change to net income.

(viii) Discontinued operations

Under US GAAP income from discontinued operations would have been reported as a separate component of income before extraordinary items.

(ix) Foreign currency translation

BA adjusts the cost of certain aircraft which have been financed in part by loans and finance leases in foreign currency to take account of the sterling cost of related repayments during the period and the translation of outstanding liabilities on such foreign currency borrowings at the period end rate of exchange or the appropriate forward rate where liabilities have been covered forward. The depreciation charge on such aircraft is computed on such translated amounts and the adjustments to accumulated depreciation at the beginning of the period are taken to retained earnings. This accounting treatment is adopted in order to reflect the sterling cost to BA of its investment in such aircraft and as a result to match the depreciation charge more accurately with revenue.

Under US GAAP the exchange adjustments made to the cost of aircraft are required to be treated as exchange gains or losses and included in the determination of net income. The cost of the related aircraft would be fixed in pounds sterling at the rate of exchange ruling at the date of the original acquisition or lease.

ACCOUNTING FOR PENSIONS

BA has not applied the provisions of FAS 87 'Employers' accounting for pensions', which is effective for pension plans outside the US for fiscal years beginning after 15 December 1988. The effect that the implementation of this statement would have on BA's US GAAP information has not yet been quantified.

The estimated effects of the significant adjustments to income before extraordinary items and net income and to shareholders' equity which would be required if US GAAP were to be applied instead of accounting principles generally accepted in the UK, are summarised below.

Net income under US GAAP for the year ended 31 March 1988

	1988 £m	Group 1987 £m
Income (loss) before extraordinary items as reported in the consolidated statements of income		
Continuing activities	151	150
Discontinued activities		(2)
	151	148
Estimated adjustments		
Depreciation		
Goodwill	(2)	
Fleet	5	6
Property	2	3
Other income (charges)		
Exchange gains (losses)		
Arising on translation of cost of aircraft	13	16
Arising on revaluation of forward exchange contracts	(21)	(8)
Surplus on disposal of tangible fixed assets and investments	1	6
Extraordinary items		4
Deferred taxation	19	(20)
	17	7
Estimated income before cumulative effect of change in accounting principle as adjusted to accord with US GAAP	168	155
Estimated cumulative effect on prior years (to 31 March 1987) of adopting FAS 96	18	
Estimated net income as adjusted to accord with US GAAP	186	155

	Pence	Pence
Per Ordinary Share as so adjusted		
Income before cumulative effect of change in		
accounting principle	23.3	21.5
Cumulative effect on prior years (to 31 March		
1987) of adopting FAS 96	2.5	
Net income	25.8	21.5
Per American Depositary Share as so adjusted		
Income before cumulative effect of change in		
accounting principle	233	215
Cumulative effect on prior years (to 31 March		
1987) of adopting FAS 96	25	
Net income	258	215

Shareholders' equity under US GAAP at 31 March 1988

	1988 £m	Group 1987 £m
Shareholders' equity as reported in the consolidated balance sheets	633	605
Estimated adjustments		
Intangible assets		
Goodwill	361	
Tangible assets		
Fleet	(306)	(41)
Property	(15)	(18)
Current liabilities		
Proposed dividend	34	30
Deferred losses on forward exchange contracts	(13)	(10)
Long-term liabilities		
Deferred losses on forward exchange contracts	(19)	(1)
Provisions for liabilities and charges:		
Deferred taxation	(124)	(155)
	(82)	(195)
Estimated shareholders' equity as adjusted to accord with US GAAP	551	410

III. CAUSES AND GROUPINGS OF INTERNATIONAL DIFFERENCES

Introduction

In the previous chapter many important differences between UK and US accounting were examined. Nevertheless, it will become clear in this chapter that, in a world context, UK and US accounting are similar. For example, it is much harder to understand and to adjust for differences within Europe.

From the Anglo-American base established in Chapter II, we will now explore the accounting of many other important countries. In this chapter, there is an investigation of the major influences creating international differences. Also, there is a suggestion about how countries might be put into groups by their similarities in accounting.

There seems to be some consensus about which factors are involved in shaping financial reporting. Those which are seen as influencing accounting development include commercial factors, such as the prevalent providers of finance and the influence of taxation.

On a worldwide scale, factors like language or geography might be thought to be relevant. However, to the extent that these **do** have some explanatory power, it seems more sensible to assume that this results from autocorrelation. That is, the fact that Australian accounting bears a marked resemblance to New Zealand accounting might be 'confirmed' by language and geographical factors. However, most of their similarities were probably **caused** not by these factors but by their historical connection with the UK, which passed on both accounting and language and was colonising most parts of Australasia in the same period.

The analysis here will be confined to the developed world. If we wanted to go beyond that, it would be necessary to include factors concerning the state of development of the economy and the nature of the political economy of the countries concerned. Of course, to some extent a precise definition of terms might make it clear that it was impossible to include some such countries. For example, if our interest is in the financial reporting practices of listed corporations, those countries with few or no such corporations have to be excluded. Fortunately, as our main purpose does concern Western countries, there is a reasonable degree of homogeneity, in that they all have developed economies, democratic governments, listed companies, qualified accountants and so on. For our purposes, the following six factors may cumulate to a powerful explanation of the differences in financial reporting: providers of finance, taxation, legal systems, the accountancy profession, conceptual bases and accidents.

The prevalent types of business organisation and ownership differ inter- **Providers of**
nationally. It will be useful at this point to discuss the nature of companies. **finance**
The great bulk of business is handled by limited companies, the most
common forms of which are the public company and the private company.
The general distinction is that only for public companies is there allowed
to be a market in their securities, such as a listing on a stock exchange.
The names for these two types of companies in some European countries
are shown in Table 8.

Public companies are less numerous than private companies, and the
laws relating to them are stricter. For example, public companies have
more onerous requirements relating to minimum capital and to profit
distribution. A further difference in 'Roman law' countries is that public
companies tend to have bearer shares, as opposed to registered shares.
This means that there is often no share register. Public companies may
then be literally anonymous (*anonyme*) or nameless (*naamloze*).

In France and Italy, capital provided by the state or by banks is very
significant, as are small and large family businesses. In Germany, the
banks in particular are important owners of companies as well as
providers of debt finance. A majority of shares in some public companies
are owned or controlled as proxies by banks, particularly by the Deutsche,
Dresdner and Commerz Banks. The importance of banks is increased by
the prevalence of bearer shares (mentioned above). In Germany, for
example, shareholders are required to deposit their valuable bearer
share certificates with their bank, which then collects dividends and
exercises proxy votes. As a result of this multi-faceted influence, banks
are often represented on boards of directors.

By contrast, British or American companies tend to be funded by share

TABLE 8.	NAMES FOR PRIVATE AND PUBLIC COMPANIES	
Country	*Private company*	*Public company*
France, Luxembourg, Belgium	Société à responsibilité limitée (Sàrl)	Société anonyme (SA)
Italy	Società a responsabilità limitata (Srl)	Società per azioni (SpA)
Netherlands	Besloten vennootschap (BV)	Naamloze vennoot- schap (NV)
Spain	Sociedad de responsibilidad limitada (SRL)	Sociedad anónima (SA)
UK, Ireland	Private limited company (Ltd)	Public limited company (PLC)
Germany	Gesellschaft mit beschränkter Haftung (GmbH)	Aktiengesellschaft (AG)

TABLE 9. CHARACTERISATION OF CORPORATE FINANCING AND USERS OF ACCOUNTS

Widespread shares, outside creditors	*Banks, governments, families*
UK	Germany
Ireland	France
Netherlands	Belgium
US	Italy
Canada	Spain
Australia	Portugal
New Zealand	Greece
	Switzerland
	Sweden

TABLE 10.   **MAJOR STOCK EXCHANGES 1988–1989**

Country	*Exchange companies*	*Domestic companies (over 200) 1988*	*Market capitalisation end June 1989 (£ million)*	*Market capitalisation as % of UK*
Europe				
Denmark	Copenhagen	290	58,706	13
France	Paris	459	157,000	35
Germany	Federation of Exchanges	609	171,000	39
Italy	Milan	228	89,355	20
Luxembourg	Luxembourg	422	n/a	n/a
Netherlands	Amsterdam	232	81,330	18
Spain	Madrid	369	66,108	15
UK	ISE	1,804	443,265	100
North America				
Canada	Toronto	1,147	189,146	43
USA	NASDAQ	4,179	229,229	52
	NYSE	1,604	1,787,892	403
Asia-Pacific				
Australia	Association of Exchanges	1,393	78,328	18
Hong Kong	Hong Kong	282	54,339	12
Japan	Tokyo	1,571	2,326,396	525

Source: based on *Quality of Markets Quarterly*, ISE, London, Autumn 1989.

finance and to have lower gearing. Furthermore, the share finance is very widely spread, particularly compared with continental Europe. The country with the longest history of 'public' companies is The Netherlands. Although it has a fairly small stock exchange, shares in many large companies are widely held and actively traded.

A classification of countries on this basis would be as shown in Table 9. Evidence that this characterisation is reasonable may be found by looking at the number of listed companies in various countries. Table 10 shows the numbers of domestic listed shares on stock exchanges where there are over 200 such companies. A comparison between the UK and Germany or France is instructive. A two-group categorisation of these countries fits reasonably with the classification just shown.

Upon closer examination, the split between the UK type and the continental type is even starker than this table of listed companies suggests. First, the continental European (and South American and Japanese) numbers are misleadingly high because of the importance of 'insider' owners, non-voting and preference shares, and cross-holdings. Secondly, the UK/US numbers need to have added to them the figures for unlisted markets and over-the-counter stocks.

My suggestion from this is that, in countries with a widespread ownership of companies by shareholders who do not have access to internal information, there will be a pressure for disclosure, audit and 'fair' information. Although it is to some extent the case that shares in countries like the UK and the USA are held by institutional investors rather than by individual shareholders, this still contrasts with state, bank or family holdings. Indeed, the increased importance of institutional investors is perhaps a reinforcement for the suggestion. Institutional investors hold larger blocks of shares and may be better organised than private shareholders. Thus their desire for information and their command of resources should increase this pressure, although they may also be able successfully to press for more detailed information than is generally available to the public.

Fairness

'Fair', as used above, needs to be defined. It is a concept related to those large number of outside owners who require unbiased information about the success of the business and its state of affairs. Fairness implies that the accounting information will be in accordance with commercial reality and will not be misleading. Although reasonable prudence will be expected, these shareholders are interested in comparing one year with another and one company with another; thus the accruals concept and some degree of realism will be required. This entails judgement, which entails experts. This expertise is also required for the checking of the financial statements by auditors. In countries like the UK and The Netherlands, over many decades this can result in a tendency to require accountants to work out their own technical rules. This is acceptable to governments because of the influence and expertise of the accountancy profession, which is usually running ahead of the interests of the government (in its capacity as shareholder, protector of the public interest or collector of taxes). Thus 'generally accepted accounting principles' control accounting. To the extent that governments intervene, they impose disclosure, filing or measurement requirements which tend to follow best practice rather than to create it.

In other European countries, banks, governments or families will nominate directors. Thus the major providers of finance have rapid access to detailed financial information. The traditional paucity of 'outsider' shareholders has meant that external financial reporting has been largely invented for the purposes of governments, as tax collectors or controllers of the economy. This has not encouraged the development of flexibility, judgement, fairness or experimentation.

Variation in audit and publication

So, as a counter to the above hypothesis, it may be suggested that, in countries of continental Europe where most companies are heavily influenced by 'insiders', there will be little pressure for published accounts or for external audit. This is approximately true in Europe. For example, about a million companies had to publish audited accounts in the UK, whereas only public companies (i.e. about 2,200 AGs) and a few other very large companies had to do so in Germany. Audit and publication were extended in Germany for 1987 year ends as a result of the EC's Fourth Directive. However, even then many private companies disobeyed the instruction to have auditors and to publish annual reports.

Control of markets in France and Italy

Despite this great distinction, governments in most continental countries have recognised their responsibility to require public or listed companies to publish audited financial statements. This happened in a 1965 Act in West Germany. In France and Italy the government has set up bodies specifically to control the securities markets: in France the Commission des Opérations de Bourse (COB), and in Italy the Commissione Nazionale per le Società e la Borsa (CONSOB). These bodies are to some extent modelled on the Securities and Exchange Commission (SEC) of the USA. They have been associated with important developments in financial reporting, generally in the direction of Anglo-American practice. This is not surprising, as these stock exchange bodies are taking the part of private and institutional shareholders who have, over a much longer period, helped to shape Anglo-American accounting systems.

In France, COB was formed in 1968. Its officers are appointed by the government. It is charged with encouraging the growth of the Bourse by improving the quality of published information and the operations of the market. It has established listing requirements and has investigated cases of non-compliance with publication and disclosure requirements. Perhaps its most obvious campaign was that to introduce consolidation. In 1968 consolidation was extremely rare, even for listed companies. Matters improved substantially under pressure from COB, including a requirement to consolidate for all companies wishing to obtain a new listing.

Although there are far fewer listed companies in Italy than there are in France (see Table 10), the effect of CONSOB may be even greater than that of COB, partly because of the much less satisfactory state of affairs in Italy before CONSOB's formation in June 1974. CONSOB has powers to call for consolidation or extra disclosures which it has not used extensively yet. However, its real influence is linked to Presidential Decree 126 of March 1975 which, after much delay, was introduced by statutory instrument. This requires listed companies to have a more extensive audit, undertaken by an auditing company approved by CONSOB. This requirement is in addition to the statutory audit by *sindaci* or state registered auditors.

TABLE 11.		EC CORPORATION TAX SYSTEMS		
Country	Imputation introduced	National corporation tax (CT) rate (%)	Tax credit as percentage of dividend	Tax credit as percentage of underlying CT
Belgium	1963	43	50	66.3
France	1965	45	50	61.1
UK	1973	35	37.0 (i.e. 27/73)	68.7
Ireland	1976	50	53.8 (i.e. 35/65)	53.8
Germany	1977	56, 36	56.25	100.0
Denmark	1977	50	25	25.0
Italy	1977	46	56.25	78.3
Greece	Div. deductible	49	–	–
Portugal	Split rate	52, 40	–	–
Luxembourg	Classical	57	–	–
Netherlands	Classical	42	–	–
Spain	Classical	35	–	–

Taxation

Although it is possible to make groupings of tax systems in a number of ways, only some of them are of relevance to financial reporting. For example, it is easy to divide EC countries into those using 'classical' and those using 'imputation' systems of corporation tax, as in Table 11.

This distinction, however, does not affect financial reporting. What is much more relevant is the degree to which taxation regulations determine accounting measurements. To some extent this can be revealed in a negative way by studying the problem of deferred taxation, which is caused by timing differences between tax and accounting treatments. In the UK, the USA and The Netherlands, for example, the problem of deferred tax has caused much controversy and a considerable amount of accounting standard documentation (see Chapter II).

By contrast, in France or Germany the problem does not really exist to be solved; for in these countries it is to a large extent the case that the tax rules **are** the accounting rules. In Germany, the commercial accounts (*Handelsbilanz*) should be the same as the tax accounts (*Steuerbilanz*). There is even a word for this idea: the *Massgeblichkeitsprinzip* (principle of bindingness).

Tax and depreciation

One obvious example of the effects of this concerns depreciation. In the UK, the amount of depreciation charged in the published financial statements is determined according to custom established over the last century and influenced by the accounting standard SSAP 12. The standard points out that:

> Depreciation should be allocated to accounting periods so as to charge a fair proportion of cost or valuation of the asset to each accounting period expected to benefit from its use (para 3) . . . Management should select the method regarded as most appropriate to the type of asset and its use in the business so as to allocate depreciation as fairly as possible (para 8).

These injunctions are of a fairly general nature, and their spirit is quite frequently ignored. Convention and pragmatism, rather than exact rules or even the spirit of the standard, also determine the method of judging the scrap value and the expected length of life.

The amount of depreciation **for tax purposes** in the UK is quite independent of these figures. It is determined by capital allowances, which are a formalised scheme of tax depreciation allowances designed to standardise the amounts allowed and to act as investment incentives. Because of the separation of the two schemes there can be a complete lack of subjectivity in tax allowances but full room for judgement in financial depreciation charges.

At the opposite extreme, in countries like Germany, the tax regulations lay down depreciation rates to be used for particular assets. These are generally based on the expected useful lives of assets. However, in some cases, accelerated depreciation allowances are available: for example, for industries producing energy-saving or anti-pollution products or, in the past, for those operating in West Berlin or other areas bordering East Germany. If these allowances are to be claimed for tax purposes (which would normally be sensible), they must be charged in the financial accounts. Thus, the charge against profit would be said by a UK accountant not to be 'fair', even though it could certainly be 'correct' or 'legal'. This influence is felt even in the details of the choice of method of depreciation, as shown by an extract from the Annual Report of AEG Telefunken for 1986 (p. 23):

> Plant and machinery are depreciated over a useful life of ten years on a declining balance basis; straight-line depreciation is adopted as soon as this results in a higher charge.

Tax and asset valuation

A second example of the overriding effect of taxation on accounting measurement is the valuation of fixed assets in France. During the inflationary 1970s and before, French companies were allowed to revalue assets. However, this would have entailed extra taxation owing to the increase in the post-revaluation balance sheet total compared with the previous year's. Consequently, except in the special case of merger by *fusion* when tax-exempt revaluation is allowed, revaluation was not practised. However, the Finance Acts of 1978 and 1979 made revaluation obligatory for listed companies and for those which solicit funds from the public; it was optional for others. The purpose was to show balance sheets more realistically. The revaluation was performed by the use of government indices relating to 31 December 1976. The credit went to an undistributable revaluation reserve. As a result of this, for depreciable assets, an amount equal to the extra depreciation due to revaluation is credited each year to profit and loss and **debited** to the revaluation account. Thus the effect of revaluation on profit (**and tax**) is neutralised. This move from no revaluations to compulsory revaluations was due to the change in tax rules. The effects have spilled over into the 1990s.

Somewhat similar tax-based revaluations have occurred in Italy and Spain. Further examples of the influence of tax are easy to find: bad debt provisions (determined by tax laws in many continental countries); development and maintenance expenditures (carried forward for tax purposes in Spain); or various provisions related to specific industries (see the discussion of provisions and reserves in Chapter IV).

The effects of all this are to reduce the room for the operation of the accruals convention (which is the driving force behind such practices as depreciation) and to reduce 'fairness'. Until the legislation following the EC's Fourth Directive, the importance of these tax effects was not disclosed in published accounts. With some variations, this *Massgeblichkeitsprinzip* operates in most continental countries except for The Netherlands and Denmark. It is perhaps due partly to the pervasive influence of codification in law, and partly to the predominance of taxation as a cause of accounting.

The alternative approach is found in countries such as the UK, Ireland and The Netherlands, which have an older tradition of published accounting where commercial rules came first. Most of the countries on the left side of Table 12 are, in varying degrees, like this.

In most cases, there is not the degree of separation between tax and financial reporting that is found in the UK in the shape of capital allowances. However, in all such countries the taxation authorities have to adjust the commercial accounts for their own purposes, after exerting only minor influences directly on them. One major US exception to this (LIFO) was discussed in the previous chapter.

Legal systems   Roman law

Most European countries have a system of law which is based on the Roman *jus civile*, as compiled by Justinian in the sixth century and developed by European universities from the twelfth century. Here rules are linked to ideas of justice and morality; they become doctrine. The word 'codified' may be associated with such a system. This difference has the

TABLE 12.	TAX RULES AND ACCOUNTING
Little direct influence of tax rules on accounting	*Heavy influence of tax rules on accounting*
UK	Germany
Ireland	Japan
Netherlands	Belgium
US	Italy
Canada	Spain
Australia	Portugal
New Zealand	Greece
Hong Kong	Switzerland
Singapore	Sweden

important effect that company law or commercial codes need to establish rules in detail for accounting and financial reporting. For example, in The Netherlands, accounting law is contained in Book 2 of the Civil Code; in Germany and France, the Commercial Code contains accounting rules which are supplemented by company law and, in France, by a government-controlled accounting plan (see Table 13).

English law

On the other hand, the UK and Ireland have a commercial legal system which has relied upon a limited amount of statute law. This is because the environment has been the 'common law' system that was formed in England primarily by post-Conquest judges acting on the sovereign's behalf. It is less abstract than codified law; a common law rule seeks to provide an answer to a specific case rather than to formulate a general rule for the future. Although this common law system originated in England, it may be found in similar forms in many countries influenced by England. Thus the federal law of the USA, and the laws of India, Australia and so on, are to a greater or lesser extent modelled on English common law. This system naturally influences company law, which traditionally does not prescribe a large number of detailed all-embracing rules to cover the behaviour of companies and how they should publish their financial statements. To a large extent, accounting within such a context is not dependent upon law. This was certainly the case in the UK until the Companies Act 1981 introduced rules from an EC Directive based on German law.

Accounting plans

As has been mentioned, regulation in some 'Roman' countries is achieved partly through accounting plans, which include uniform formats for accounts. It was for internal, cost accounting purposes that uniform formats were first developed in Germany. They could also be used for inter-firm comparisons within an industry. In France, the needs of the Economics Ministry in its role as controller of the French economy were seen to be well served by the use of uniform accounting, encouraged by the occupying German forces in the early 1940s. Consequently, such a system has been in use in France throughout the post-war years. The first full version of the *plan comptable général* was produced in 1947, and revised versions were issued in 1957 and (as a partial implementation of the Fourth Directive) in 1982. The *plan* exists in many versions for different industries. It comprises a chart of accounts, definitions of terms, model financial statements and rules for measurement and valuation.

The chart of accounts controls a company's internal bookkeeping

TABLE 13.

EXTRACT FROM FRENCH CHART OF ACCOUNTS

Balance sheet accounts | *Management accounts*

Class 1 Capital accounts (capital loans and similar creditors)	Class 2 Fixed asset accounts	Class 3 Stock and work-in-progress accounts	Class 4 Personal accounts	Class 5 Financial accounts	Class 6 Expense accounts	Class 7 Income accounts	Class 8 Special accounts	Class 9 Cost accounts
10 Capital and reserves	20 Intangible assets	30	40 Suppliers and related accounts	50 Trade investments	60 Purchases and stock movements (supplies and goods for resale)	70 Sales of goods and services	80 Contingent assets and liabilities	90 Reciprocal accounts
11 Profit or loss brought forward	21 Tangible assets	31 Raw materials	41 Trade debtors and related accounts	51 Banks, financial and similar institutions	61 Purchases from subcontractors and external charges (related to investment)	71 Movements in finished goods during the accounting period	81	91 Cost reclassifications
12 Profit or loss for the financial year	22 Fixed assets under concession	32 Other consumables	42 Employees and related accounts	52	62 Other external charges (related to operations)	72 Work performed by the undertaking for its own purposes and capitalised	82	92 Cost analysis centres
13 Investment grants	23 Fixed assets in course of construction	33 Work-in-progress (goods)	43 Social security and other public agencies	53 Cash in hand	63 Taxes, direct and indirect	73 Net income recognised on long-term contracts	83	93 Manufacturing costs
14 Provisions created for tax purposes	24	34 Work-in-progress (services)	44 The government and other public bodies	54 Imprest accounts and credits	64 Staff costs	74 Operating subsidies	84	94 Stocks
15 Provisions for liabilities and charges	25	35 Finished goods	45 Accounts current – group companies and proprietors	55	65 Other operating charges	75 Other operating income	85	95 Cost of goods sold

16 Loans and similar creditors	26 Participating interests and debts relating thereto	36	46 Sundry debtors and creditors	56	66 Financial costs	76 Financial income	86 Intra-company exchanges of goods and services (charges)	96 Standard cost variances
17 Debts related to participating interests	27 Other financial assets	37 Goods for resale	47 Suspense accounts	57 Internal transfers	67 Extraordinary	77 Extraordinary	87 Intra-company exchanges of goods and services (income)	97 Difference in accounting treatments
18 Branch and inter-company accounts	28 Provisions for depreciation of fixed assets	38	48 Prepayments and accruals	58	68 Depreciation amortisation, transfers to	78 Depreciation and provisions written back	88	98 Manufacturing profit and loss account
19	29 Provisions for loss in value of fixed assets	39 Provisions for loss in value of stocks and work-in-progress	49 Provisions for loss in value on personal accounts	59 Provisions for loss in value on financial accounts	69 Profit sharing by employees, taxes on profits and similar items	79 Charges transferred	89	99 Internal transfers

system. It is a decimalised system of nominal ledger codes. The first two digits of the current French chart are shown in Table 13. However, the detail goes down to five digits. This system makes work easier for auditors, tax inspectors and accountants as they move from one company to another. It also speeds the training of bookkeepers; and it has obvious microcomputer application.

The influence of the *plan comptable* is all-pervasive. The chart must be completed each year for national statistical purposes; the tax returns are based on the *plan*; published financial statements use the model formats (see Chapter IV); and all the former use the standard definitions and measurement rules. The *plan* even stretches to cost and management accounting. Its usefulness for central statistical purposes is very obvious. A government economist in Paris can collect charts for all companies and add together all amounts under a particular decimalised code in order to find the total investment in a particular type of fixed asset, defined in a standardised way. Naturally, as the government is historically the main user of accounting information in its capacities as economic controller, tax collector and provider of state capital, the *plan* is controlled by a government body: the Conseil National de la Comptabilité. It is enforced through a company law of 1983.

In Belgium, part of the process of preparing for the implementation of the Fourth Directive during the 1970s was the introduction of an accounting plan in 1976, not dissimilar from the French one. The Belgians had used a chart of accounts for some industries during the inter-war years, and had experienced full use of it during the early 1940s. The *plan comptable minimum normalisé* is now compulsory. However, unlike the French *plan*, the Belgian one mainly concerns charts of accounts, which are to be sent to the Banque Nationale.

In Spain, an accounting plan has been progressively introduced. The Ministry of Public Finance established the Institute of Accounting Planning in 1973, which has produced several versions of the plan for different sectors. As in France, the plan consists of a chart of accounts, a set of definitions, formats for annual accounts and valuation principles. The headings of the decimalised chart of accounts are in the same order as in the French chart, though the subheadings vary to some extent. The plan began by being voluntary. Then, by an Act of December 1973, the plan had to be used for those companies who wished to revalue. This continued for the 1978 and 1979 fiscal revaluations (somewhat like the French revaluations of similar date). However, by an Order of 14 January 1980, companies covered by plans already in issue must now comply with the plans.

Greece has also adopted an accounting plan. In Greece, France and Spain, the plans include uniform financial statements for publication. In Belgium and Germany, uniform financial statements are required instead by company law. An interesting irony is that Germany is now the only country of the five not to have a compulsory accounting plan.

In Anglo-Saxon countries, there has generally been much less uniformity. As far as formats for financial statements are concerned, there were no rules in law (before the 1981 UK Act and the 1983 Netherlands Act) and virtually none in accounting standards. The requirements of the Fourth Directive were based on German law and were revolutionary compared with previous Anglo-Dutch rules. But even now, there remains much more flexibility in the UK, Ireland and The Netherlands than in the rest of the EC. In the USA and Canada, formats are not fixed, although there are compulsory formats in Australian company law.

Accounting standards

Turning to accounting principles, the control by company law, tax law or accounting plan has been substantial in most EC countries. Again, by contrast, in the UK, Ireland and The Netherlands there have traditionally been no rules in company law apart from 'fairness'. Instead, the accountancy profession has been influential in inventing and policing the rules of valuation and measurement. In the UK and Ireland, the Accounting Standards Committee was controlled by the professional bodies, although an independent Accounting Standards Board took over in 1990. In The Netherlands, guidelines are published by the Council for Annual Reporting (Raad voor Jaarrekening) in which the Netherlands Institute of Registered Accountants plays the most influential role.

Standards and guidelines in these latter countries are not legally binding. In the UK and Ireland, non-compliance should lead to an audit qualification; in The Netherlands, not even that. However, the legal requirement for 'fairness' would be likely to be interpreted by a court with the aid of standards. In The Netherlands there is an Enterprise Chamber of the Court of Justice especially for accounting cases.

TABLE 14.	SOME LEGAL SYSTEMS
Common law	*Roman, codified*
England and Wales	France
Ireland	Italy
United States	Germany
Canada	Spain
Australia	Netherlands
New Zealand	Japan (commercial)

Note: the laws of Scotland, Israel, South Africa, Quebec, Louisiana and the Philippines embody elements of both systems.

In other English-speaking countries, there are also accounting standards set by non-governmental bodies. In the USA, the Financial Accounting Standards Board, which is independent from both government and the profession, sets standards which are enforced by the SEC. In Australia and Canada, the profession sets the standards but governments are involved in overseeing and enforcing. In New Zealand the arrangements are similar to those formerly operating in the UK.

There has been plenty of room for variety in those Anglo-Saxon countries in the EC. However, the implementation of the Fourth Directive has introduced many detailed rules into law for the first time. This has somewhat increased uniformity, but mainly it has raised problems between law and standards.

The difference in legal traditions means that accounting rules tend to be law based and slow to change in 'Roman' countries, whereas the detail is controlled by accountants in 'English' countries. This affects both the nature of regulation and the nature of the detailed rules in a country. Table 14 illustrates the way in which some countries' legal systems divide between these two types. Notice the similarity with the earlier tables on company finance and tax.

The profession   The strength, size and competence of the accountancy profession in a country may follow to a large extent from the various factors outlined above and from the type of financial reporting they have helped to produce. For example, the lack of a substantial body of private shareholders and public companies in some countries means that the need for auditors is much smaller than it is in the UK or the USA. However, the nature of the profession also feeds back into the type of accounting that is practised and **could** be practised. For example, as has been mentioned, the 1975 Decree in Italy (not brought into effect until the 1980s) requiring listed companies to have extended audits similar to those operated in the UK could only be brought into effect initially because of the substantial presence of international accounting firms. This constitutes a considerable obstacle to any attempts at significant and deep harmonisation of accounting between some countries. The need for extra auditors was a controversial issue in Germany's implementation of the EC's Fourth Directive.

The scale of the differences is illustrated in Table 15, which lists the bodies whose members may audit the accounts of companies (but see below for an explanation of the French and German situation). These remarkable figures need some interpretation. For example, let us carefully compare the German with the British figures. In Germany, there is a separate though overlapping profession of tax experts (*Steuerberater*), which is larger than the accountancy body. However, in the UK the

TABLE 15.	ACCOUNTANCY BODIES, AGE AND SIZE		
Country	Body	Founding date*	Approximate number of members, 1987–8 (thousand)
United States	American Institute of Certified Public Accountants	1887	264
Canada	Canadian Institute of Chartered Accountants	1902 (1880)	44
United Kingdom and Ireland	Institute of Chartered Accountants in England and Wales	1880 (1870)	85
	Institute of Chartered Accountants of Scotland	1951 (1854)	12
	Chartered Association of Certified Accountants	1939 (1891)	30
	Institute of Chartered Accountants in Ireland	1888	6
Australia	Australian Society of Accountants	1952 (1887)	55
	Institute of Chartered Accountants in Australia	1928 (1886)	17
New Zealand	New Zealand Society of Accountants	1909 (1894)	15
Netherlands	Nederlands Instituut van Register-accountants	1895	6
France	Ordre des Experts Comptables et des Comptables Agréés	1942	11
Germany	Institut der Wirtschaftsprüfer	1932	5
Japan	Japanese Institute of Certified Public Accountants	1948	10

*Dates of earliest predecessor bodies in brackets.

'accountants' figure is especially inflated by the inclusion of many who specialise in or occasionally practice in tax. Secondly, a German accountant may only be a member of the Institut if he is in practice, whereas at least half of the British figure represents members in commerce, industry, government, education and so on. Thirdly, the training period is much longer in Germany than it is in the UK or, particularly, the US. It normally involves a four-year relevant degree course, six years practical experience (four in the profession), and a professional examination consisting of oral and written tests plus a thesis. This tends to last until the aspiring accountant is 30 to 35 years old. Thus, many of the German 'students' would be counted as part of the qualified figure if they were in the British or American system. In addition, in the late 1980s Germany resuscitated a second-tier auditing body for the audit of private companies, the Vereidigte Buchprüfer.

These factors help to explain the differences. However, there is still a very substantial residual difference which results from the much larger number of companies to be audited and the different process of forming a judgement on the 'fair' view.

Government influence

It is interesting to note a further division along Anglo-American versus Franco-German lines. In the former countries, governments or government agencies do require certain types of companies to be audited, and put certain limits on who shall be auditors, with government departments having the final say. However, in general, membership of the private professional accountancy bodies is the method of registering as an auditor. On the other hand, in France and Germany there is a dual set of accountancy bodies. Those in Table 15 are not the bodies to which one must belong to act as an auditor of companies, though to a large extent the membership of these professional qualifying bodies overlaps with the auditing regulatory bodies (see Table 16), and membership of the former enables membership of the latter.

The professional bodies set qualifying exams, consider ethical matters, belong to the international accountancy bodies and so on. The auditing

TABLE 16.	ACCOUNTING BODIES IN FRANCE AND GERMANY	
	Private professional body	*State auditing body*
France	Ordre des Experts Comptables	Compagnie Nationale des Commissaires aux Comptes
Germany	Institut der Wirtschaftsprüfer	Wirtschaftsprüferkammer

bodies are run by the state. The Compagnie Nationale is responsible to the Ministry of Justice; the Wirtschaftsprüferkammer to the Federal Minister of Economics. This dual system was introduced in the UK by the Companies Act 1989, which implemented the EC's Eighth Directive. However, in the UK the same accountancy bodies are allowed to act as qualifying and regulatory bodies.

There has also been a strong influence in a few cases from theory, perhaps most obviously in the case of microeconomics in The Netherlands. Accounting theorists there (notably Theodore Limperg Jr) had advanced the case that the users of financial statements would be given the fairest view of the performance and state of affairs of an individual company by allowing accountants to use judgement, in the context of that particular company, to select and present accounting figures. In particular, it was suggested that replacement cost information might give the best picture. The looseness of law and tax requirements, and the receptiveness of the profession to microeconomic ideas (no doubt partly because of their training by the academic theorists), have led to the present diversity of practice, the emphasis on 'fairness' through judgement, and the experimentation with and practice of replacement cost accounting.

Theoretical framework

In other countries, particularly in the English-speaking world, accounting practices seem to operate and develop without a clear theoretical framework.

Inflation

Accountants in the English-speaking world and governments in continental Europe have proved remarkably immune to inflation when it comes to decisive action. However, there are other countries where inflation has been overwhelming. In several South American countries, the most obvious feature of accounting practices is the use of methods of general price level adjustment. The use of this comparatively simple method is probably due to the reasonable correlation of inflation with any particular specific price changes when the former is in hundreds of per cent per year; to the objective nature of government published indices; and to the paucity of well-trained accountants.

Without reference to inflation, it would not be possible to explain accounting differences in several countries severely affected by it. However, this factor is of little assistance in explaining accounting differences in Europe. Nevertheless, the valuation of fixed assets in particular has been affected by it in some European countries, as discussed in Chapter IV.

Accidents

Many other influences have been at work in shaping accounting practices. Some are not indirect and subtle like the type of ownership of companies, but direct and external to accounting like the framing of a law in response to economic or political events. As discussed in the previous chapter, the economic crisis in the USA in the late 1920s and early 1930s produced the Securities and Exchange Acts, which diverted US accounting from its previous course by introducing extensive disclosure requirements and control (usually by threat only) of accounting standards. As other examples, the introductions into Italy of Anglo-American accounting principles by choice of the government, and into Luxembourg of consolidation and detailed disclosure as a result of EC Directives, are against all previous trends in those countries. In Spain, the 'artificial' adoption of the accounting plan from France followed that latter country's adoption of it under the influence of the occupying Germans in the early 1940s.

Perhaps most obvious and least natural is the adoption of various British Companies Acts or of International Accounting Standards by developing countries with a negligible number of the sort of public companies or private shareholders which have given rise to the financial reporting practices contained in these laws and standards. In its turn, the UK in 1981 enacted uniform formats derived from the 1965 Aktiengesetz of West Germany because of EC requirements. For their part, Roman law countries are now having to grapple with the 'true and fair view' (see Chapter IV).

Putting countries into groups

So far, this chapter has discussed the causes of international differences in financial reporting practices. From this it is clear that, although no two countries have identical rules and practices, some countries seem to form pairs or larger groupings with reasonably similar influences on financial reporting. If this is so, it may be possible to establish a classification. Such an activity is a basic step in many disciplines other than accounting. Before attempting an international accounting classification, it may be useful to make short surveys of classification in other disciplines, of the normal rules for classification, of the purposes of classification, and of previous attempts at classification in accounting.

Classification is one of the basic tools of a scientist. The Mendeleyev table of elements and the Linnaean system of classification are fundamental to chemistry and biology. Classification should sharpen description and analysis. It should reveal underlying structures and enable prediction of the properties of an element based on its place in a classification.

Different types of classification are possible, from the simplest form of dichotomous grouping (e.g. things black versus things white) or rank ordering (e.g. by height of students in a class) to more complex dimensioning (such as the periodic table) or systematising (such as the Linnaean system).

It may now be useful to examine traditional methods of classification in areas close to accounting. There have been classifications of political, economic and legal systems. For example, political systems have been grouped into political democracies, tutelary democracies, modernising oligarchies, totalitarian oligarchies and traditional oligarchies. Economic systems have been divided into capitalism, socialism, communism and fascism. A more recent classification is into traditional economies, market economies and planned economies.

One set of authors, while classifying legal systems, has supplied practical criteria for determining whether two systems are in the same group. Systems are said to be in the same group if 'someone educated in . . . one law will then be capable, without much difficulty, of handling [the other]'.[1] Also, the two systems must not be 'founded on opposed philosophical, political or economic principles'. The second criterion ensures that systems in the same group not only have similar superficial characteristics, but also have similar fundamental structures and are likely to react to new circumstances in similar ways. Using these criteria a four-group legal classification was obtained: Romano-Germanic, common law, socialist and philosophical-religious.

In all the above examples, the type of classification used was rudimentary, involving no more than splitting systems into a few groups. The groups within the classifications were sometimes not precisely defined or exhaustive. Also, the method used to determine and fill the groups was little more than subjective classification based on personal knowledge or descriptive literature. These shortcomings are very difficult to avoid because of the complexity and greyness in the social sciences.

In accounting, classification should facilitate a study of the logic of and the difficulties facing international harmonisation. Classification should also assist in the training of accountants and auditors who operate internationally. Further, a developing country might be better able to understand the available types of financial reporting, and to decide which would be most appropriate for it, by seeing which other countries use particular systems. Also, it should be possible for a country to predict the problems that it is about to face and the solutions that might work by looking at other countries in its group.

Early classifications

Early attempts at classification and more recent descriptions of different national systems form the background to modern classifications. Of the

[1] R. David and J.E.C. Brierley, *Major Legal Systems in the World Today*, Stevens, London, 1978, p. 20.

former, there is evidence for a three-group classification (UK, US and continental) being used from the beginning of the twentieth century.[2] More recent descriptions and analyses like those by Price Waterhouse (surveys of 1973, 1975 and 1979) and the AICPA (surveys of 1964 and 1975) provide the raw material for classification.

Professor Gerhard Mueller broke new ground in 1967 by preparing a suggested classification of accounting systems into four patterns of development. This was a simple grouping which is not accompanied by an explanation of the method used to obtain it. However, the 'range of four is considered sufficient to embrace accounting as it is presently known and practised in various parts of the globe'.[3] Each group was illustrated by one or two examples. It may well be that it is not reasonable to expect a more sophisticated classification, particularly in a pioneering work, and that Mueller's informed judgement was one of the best methods of classification available.

Mueller stresses that the types of accounting rules which exist in a country are a product of economic, political and other environments, which have determined the nature of the system. This also suggests that other countries' rules would not be appropriate to a particular country and that rules must be chosen to fit that country's needs. Consequently, doubt is cast on the possibility and usefulness of harmonisation.

Mueller's four patterns of development are as follows:

Accounting within a macroeconomic framework   In this case, accounting has developed as an adjunct of national economic policies. We might expect such financial accounting to stress value-added statements, to encourage income smoothing, to be equivalent to tax accounting and to include social responsibility accounting. Sweden is said to be an example.

The microeconomic approach   This approach can prosper in a market-oriented economy which has individual private businesses at the core of its economic affairs. The influence of microeconomics has led accounting to try to reflect economic reality in its measurement and valuations. This means that accounting rules must be sophisticated but flexible. Developments like replacement cost accounting will be accepted most readily in such systems. The Netherlands is suggested as an example.

Accounting as an independent discipline   Systems of this sort have developed independently of governments or economic theories. Accounting has developed in business, has faced problems when they arrived, and has adopted solutions which worked. Theory is held in little regard, and is turned to only in emergencies or used *ex post facto* in an attempt to justify practical conclusions. Expressions such as 'generally accepted

---

[2] H.R. Hatfield, 'Some variations in accounting practices in England, France, Germany and the United States', *Journal of Accounting Research*, Autumn 1966.

[3] G.G. Mueller, *International Accounting*, Macmillan, New York, 1967, p. 2.

accounting principles' are typical. Mueller recognised the accounting systems of the United Kingdom and the United States as examples.

Uniform accounting   Such systems have developed where governments have used accounting as a part of the administrative control of business. Accounting can be used to measure performance, allocate funds, assess the size of industries and resources, control prices, collect taxation, manipulate sectors of business and so on. It involves standardisation of definitions, measurements and presentation. France is cited as an example.

Mueller was classifying financial reporting systems not directly, on the basis of differences in **practices**, but indirectly, on the basis of differences in the importance of economic, governmental and business factors in the development of particular systems. However, one might expect that systems which have developed in a similar way would have similar accounting practices.

Nevertheless, there are a few problems with Mueller's classification. The fact that there are only four exclusive groups and no hierarchy reduces the usefulness of the classification. In effect The Netherlands is the only country in one of the groups, and the classification does not show whether or not Dutch accounting is closer to UK accounting than it is to Swedish accounting. Similarly, the classification cannot include such facts as that German accounting exhibits features which remind one of macro-economic accounting as well as of uniform accounting.

British Commonwealth model	Latin American model	Continental European model	United States model
Australia	Argentina	Belgium	Canada
Bahamas	Bolivia	France	Japan
Eire	Brazil	Germany	Mexico
Fiji	Chile	Italy	Panama
Jamaica	Columbia	Spain	Philippines
Kenya	Ethiopia	Sweden	United States
Netherlands	India	Switzerland	
New Zealand	Paraguay	Venezuela	
Pakistan	Peru		
Singapore	Uruguay		
South Africa			
Trinidad and Tobago			
United Kingdom			
Zimbabwe			

TABLE 17. CLASSIFICATION BASED ON 1973 MEASUREMENT PRACTICES

Source: Nair and Frank (1980), p. 429.

FIGURE 1. GROUPINGS OF SOME MAJOR COUNTRIES

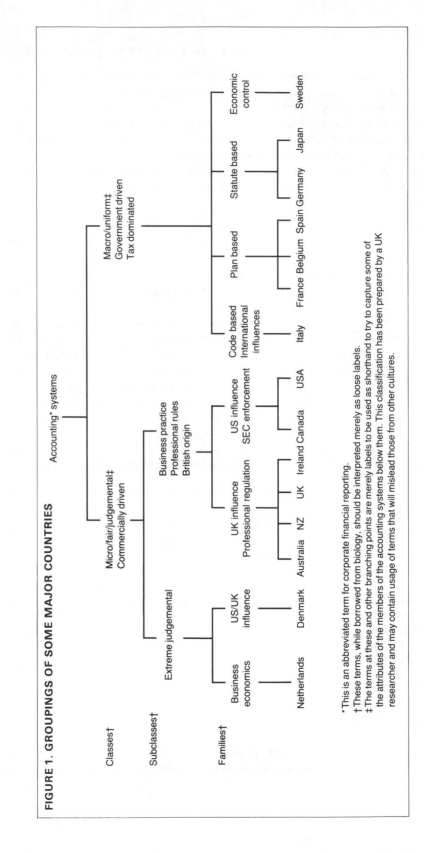

*This is an abbreviated term for corporate financial reporting.
†These terms, while borrowed from biology, should be interpreted merely as loose labels.
‡The terms at these and other branching points are merely labels to be used as shorthand to try to capture some of the attributes of the members of the accounting systems below them. This classification has been prepared by a UK researcher and may contain usage of terms that will mislead those from other cultures.

Classifications using clustering

Other researchers have used the 1973 and the 1975 Price Waterhouse surveys of practices. For example, one set of researchers[4] divides the 1973 survey's financial reporting characteristics into those relating to measurement and those relating to disclosure. This is a very useful differentiation, particularly because of the effect it has on the classification of countries like Germany which have advanced disclosure requirements. Using disclosure and measurement characteristics, Germany is classified in a 'US group'. However, by using measurement characteristics only, it is possible to classify Germany in the continental European group. Table 17 represents the classification using measurement characteristics. As yet there is no hierarchy, but the overall results do seem very plausible and fit well with the analysis in previous chapters of this book. The suggestion is that, in a worldwide context, much of continental Europe can be seen as using the same system. However, the UK, Ireland and The Netherlands are noticeably different.

A new approach to grouping countries

It would be possible to criticise the classifications discussed above for (1) lack of precision in the definition of what is to be classified; (2) lack of a model with which to compare the statistical results; (3) lack of hierarchy, which would add more subtlety to the portrayal of the size of the differences between countries; and (4) lack of judgement in the choice of 'important' discriminating features. Can these problems be remedied? The author has attempted to solve them in the following ways.

The scope of the work is defined as the classification of some Western countries by the financial reporting practices of their **public companies**. The reporting practices are those concerned with **measurement and valuation**. It is public companies whose financial statements are generally available and whose practices can be most easily discovered. It is the international differences in reporting between such companies which are of main interest to shareholders, creditors, auditing firms, taxation authorities, managements and harmonising agencies. Measurement and valuation practices were chosen because these determine the size of the figures for profit, capital, total assets, liquidity and so on. The result is Figure 1.

The figure suggests that there are two main types of financial reporting 'system': the micro/professional and the macro/uniform. The former involves accountants in individual companies striving to present fair information to outside users, without detailed constraint of law or tax rules

---

[4] R.D. Nair and W.G. Frank, 'The impact of disclosure and measurement practices in international accounting classifications', *Accounting Review*, July 1980.

but with professional guidelines. The latter type has accounting mainly as a servant of the state, particularly for taxation purposes.

The micro/professional side contains Denmark, The Netherlands, the UK, Ireland, the USA, Australia, New Zealand and Canada. The Netherlands is even more free of rules than are the UK and Ireland, although the influence of microeconomic theory has led to the use of replacement cost information to varying degrees. Denmark rearranged its accounting system after World War II in order to become more like the US or the UK.

The macro/uniform side contains all the other European countries and Japan. However, they can be divided into groups. For example, accounting plans are now the predominant source of detailed rules in France, Belgium, Spain and Greece. In Germany company law is the major authority, and has strict observance of historical cost values and tax-based depreciation. In Italy, Luxembourg and Portugal, tax rules are also a vital determinant of detailed practices. Other rules come from commercial codes rather than from accounting plans or company laws. In Sweden, the predominant influence seems to be the government as economic planner and tax collector.

The purpose of the figure is to organise countries into groups by similarities of financial reporting measurement and valuation practices. This means that a knowledge of one country enables inferences to be drawn about others. The 'distance' between two countries is suggested by how far back up the classification it is necessary to go to reach a common point. This should be useful for those accountants and auditors who have to deal with financial reports from several countries or who have to work in more than one country.

Such a classification can be borne in mind while studying detailed differences in the next chapter. It also prompts questions about whether harmonisation is desirable and possible. This is examined in Chapter VIII.

IV. SOME MAJOR TOPIC AREAS OF INTERNATIONAL DIFFERENCE

The major causal factors discussed in the previous chapter have led to important international differences in the financial reporting of companies. The differences can be seen in the valuation of assets, in the measurement of income and in the presentation, publication and audit of accounts. This chapter gives some order to the differences by combining them under four headings. Group accounting is considered in Chapter V.

For reasons discussed earlier, there is a long tradition of publication and audit in most English-speaking countries. This means that for many years it has generally been easy to obtain the accounts of listed and other public companies, and that the accounts have been independently audited. At the extreme, in the UK publication and audit are required from **all** companies (except dormant ones). Publication does not generally mean the appearance of the accounts in a 'publication', but at least the public availability of accounts in a government office and via the company itself.

Furthermore, annual reports have for long been fairly extensive documents, containing directors' reports, funds flow statements, consolidated accounts where appropriate, and detailed explanatory notes. Interim or quarterly reports are required for listed companies, as is the disclosure of data on earnings per share.

By contrast, the comparative lack of outside shareholders in continental Europe has led to a tradition of secrecy and lack of disclosure which is still clearly apparent. For example, earnings per share are not disclosed even by listed companies in most countries; consolidation is rare in many countries; audit and publication are confined to a few companies in Italy, Spain, Switzerland, Luxembourg and Portugal. In Germany, where a law of 1985 extended publication and audit to tens of thousands of medium companies, fewer than 10% of these companies have obeyed the law.

In some continental countries, such as France and Germany, information from listed companies is now substantial but, even there, funds flow statements and EPS disclosures are not required. In some other European countries reliable assessment of companies is impossible because of the lack of information. Certainly for those wishing to assess private companies, there may be no information at all.

The formats of accounts are controlled in some countries but not in others. The 1980s saw a great extension of standardisation of formats in Europe (because of the EC Fourth Directive; see Chapter VIII) and in Australia. There are some SEC rules relating to formats in the US, but none in New Zealand, Hong Kong and many other British-influenced countries. In the EC, formats are based on those found in the Fourth Directive, which can be traced to the German public companies Act of 1965.

Formats of balance sheets are generally horizontal (two sided; in French, *en tableau*) or vertical (in French, *en liste*). In most countries, items are presented in order of increasing liquidity (i.e. for assets, starting with fixed assets and ending with cash). However, in the USA the order is reversed.

To illustrate the international differences, the practices of some companies are now shown. Extract 2 (GEC) is a fairly typical UK balance sheet, based on one of the formats in the Companies Act 1985, which itself was based on the Fourth Directive. Some Irish and Dutch companies also use these formats, as do some French consolidated accounts.

Extract 3 (Total Oil) is of a standard horizontal format as used in many European countries, including all German company balance sheets and all French individual company balance sheets. Note that this presentation has more of a technical double-entry nature, and does not allow the presentation of working capital or net assets totals.

The third balance sheet illustration (Extract 4) is that of a typical US public company. The items are in the reverse order compared with those of companies in Europe. Australia has also adopted this US order. The format may, at first sight, look vertical, but it is really just a horizontal format put on to one page; no advantage is taken of the verticality in order to calculate net assets etc.

Profit and loss accounts ('income statements' in US terminology) present an even greater variety. They can, of course, be horizontal or vertical. UK, Dutch, US and German income statements are vertical, as usually are French consolidated income statements. Other countries which have few format rules tend to follow this, such as Switzerland or Sweden. However, some countries where accounts are closely controlled by rules of governments or tax authorities tend to have a two-sided format. This applies to statutory unconsolidated accounts in Italy, France and Spain.

Two vertical income statements are shown below. The first (Dutch) profit and loss account (Extract 5) is presented by stage of production. It shows cost of sales and gross profit. Expenses are combined together by functional area. The French term is *par destination*.

The second (German) statement (Extract 6) is prepared by type of expense (*par nature* in French): wages, depreciation etc. Gross profit

EXTRACT 2.   **TYPICAL UK BALANCE SHEET**

Balance sheet of GEC at 31 March 1988

	GROUP		COMPANY	
	1988	1987	1988	1987
	£ million	£ million	£ million	£ million
Fixed Assets				
Tangible assets	824.6	828.1	60.0	121.3
Investments - shares in Group companies			926.9	816.1
- other	415.2	109.1	375.9	9.6
	1,239.8	937.2	1,362.8	947.0
Current Assets				
Stocks and contracts in progress	1,251.7	1,335.2	45.7	139.0
Debtors	1,348.4	1,433.6	517.3	394.4
Investments	392.3	403.3	105.3	143.2
Cash	1,122.8	1,414.4	671.9	777.1
	4,115.2	4,586.5	1,340.2	1,453.7
Current Liabilities: amounts falling due within one year				
Debenture loans	3.2	3.0	.7	.7
Creditors	1,950.7	1,832.8	1,324.2	1,075.1
Net Current Assets	2,161.3	2,750.7	15.3	377.9
Total Assets less Current Liabilities	3,401.1	3,687.9	1,378.1	1,324.9
Liabilities: amounts falling due after one year:				
Debenture loans	48.2	44.1	10.2	6.3
Creditors	147.1	207.7	–	–
Provisions for liabilities and charges	409.6	453.7	68.1	77.8
	2,796.2	2,982.4	1,299.8	1,240.8
Capital and Reserves				
Called up share capital	133.4	133.3	133.4	133.3
Capital redemption reserve	4.0	4.0	4.0	4.0
Share premium account	12.3	9.3	12.3	9.3
Profit and loss account	2,565.5	2,748.0	1,150.1	1,094.2
Shareholders' interest	2,715.2	2,894.6	1,299.8	1,240.8
Minority interests	81.0	87.8		
	2,796.2	2,982.4	1,299.8	1,240.8

cannot be calculated under this method, because manufacturing wages and depreciation cannot be separated out. Some UK companies choose this presentation in order to reduce disclosure. This difference means that the choice of format is not merely a superficial point.

Nearly all large companies in English-speaking countries show a statement that is vertical by stage of production. Many German companies and a few UK companies use a statement like the German example shown. French companies use *par nature* (vertical for consolidated, horizontal for individual).

Shareholder orientation

Several examples have now been given to illustrate the greater degree of shareholder orientation of accounts in countries where outside shareholders have traditionally been a major source of finance. The balance sheet shown next (Extract 7) illustrates the reverse case. These are the statutory company accounts of Fiat, one of the largest and most internationally famous Italian companies. The following points suggest a lack of shareholder orientation:

- It is a two-sided balance sheet, but of such length that even this structure is unclear.
- Individual numbers run to fourteen digits, showing a lack of interest in materiality.
- 'Memorandum accounts' are shown apparently as part of the double-entry format (and they are the same on both 'sides' of the balance sheet).
- Depreciation is shown as a 'reserve' rather than as a deduction from the relevant assets.
- Bad debt provisions are also shown on the 'liabilities' side (in US terminology as 'reserve for doubtful receivables').
- Income is shown at the end of the 'liabilities' side rather than as part of equity.

Fairness

The link between the purpose of accounts and the types of format has already been examined in the previous section. There is also a link with the degree of 'fairness'. Where there is shareholder dominance and a lack of legal and tax interference in financial reporting, fairness tends to be stronger.

Formally, the requirement for accounts to 'give a true and fair view' first arrived in the UK and in the Companies Act 1947. However, the law was probably an expression of what company accountants and auditors were already doing. Those exact words appear also in laws in Ireland, Australia, New Zealand and in many other English-speaking countries.

EXTRACT 3.   **TYPICAL EUROPEAN HORIZONTAL BALANCE SHEET**

Balance sheet of Total Oil at 31 December 1988 (F thousand)

Assets

	31 December, 1988			31 December, 1987
	Gross Amounts	Depreciation and provisions	Net Amounts	Net Amounts
Fixed Assets	33 973 795	16 999 527	16 974 268	11 895 618
Intangible assets	241 492	240 888	604	604
Tangible assets	809 070	250 301	558 769	564 733
Land.	230 922		230 922	232 633
Buildings	109 696	14 734	94 962	93 737
Other tangible assets. . .	468 452	235 567	232 885	238 363
Financial assets	32 923 233	16 508 338	16 414 895	11 330 281
Shares in affiliated companies	17 637 420	6 206 390	11 431 030	7 136 955
Loans to affiliated companies	14 601 103	10 301 948	4 299 155	3 376 595
Other loans	681 719		681 719	810 402
Deposits	2 991		2 991	6 329
Current Assets	11 864 743	12 885	11 851 858	14 335 208
Stocks	20 028	462	19 566	68 032
Debtors	10 967 412	12 423	10 954 989	12 702 440
Trade debtors.	4 244 019	10 875	4 233 144	4 723 181
Other debtors	6 723 393	1 548	6 721 845	7 979 259
Marketable securities	737 517		737 517	1 428 804
Liquid assets	104 132		104 132	116 865
Regularization accounts	35 654		35 654	19 067
Prepayments	35 654		35 654	19 067
Deferred expenditure	21 697	8 351	13 346	19 733
Premiums on redeemable bonds	25 921	25 921	–	–
Difference on exchange	443 156		443 156	701 471
TOTAL	46 329 312	17 046 684	29 282 628	26 952 030

Liabilities

	31 December 1988		31 December 1987	
	Before AGM decisions	After AGM decisions	Before AGM decisions	After AGM decisions
Capital and Reserves	16 369 540	15 643 017	16 123 153	15 398 208
Issued capital	1 816 310	1 816 310	1 812 364	1 812 364
Share premium account:				
shares and converted bonds	2 970 721	2 970 721	2 958 579	2 958 579
Revaluation reserve	1 030 331	1 030 331	1 097 033	1 097 033
Legal reserve	181 236	181 632	180 404	181 236
Statutory reserves	23 046	23 046	23 046	23 046
Other reserves:				
• General reserves.	8 586 000	8 876 000	7 826 000	8 586 000
• Surplus arising on				
exchange of shares . .	14 335	14 335	14 335	14 335
Profit brought forward. . . .	725 165	730 632	829 304	725 165
Profit for the year	1 022 386	–	1 381 638	–
Legal revaluation special				
provision	10	10	450	450
Provisions for Risks and Charges	2 280 300	2 280 300	2 434 300	2 434 300
Provisions for financial				
risks	6 300	6 300	6 300	6 300
Provisions for pensions and				
similar commitments. . . .	1 254 000	1 254 000	1 058 000	1 058 000
Provisions for specific				
sectors risks.	1 020 000	1 020 000	1 370 000	1 370 000
Creditors	10 127 052	10 853 575	7 686 913	8 411 858
Financial	4 759 083	4 759 083	3 623 829	3 623 829
Convertible debenture				
loan	118 850	118 850	132 179	132 179
Other debenture loans . . .	2 774 506	2 774 506	1 835 119	1 835 119
Other loans and finance				
debts.	1 817 544	1 817 544	1 564 397	1 564 397
Bank accounts	48 183	48 183	92 134	92 134
Operating	5 361 985	6 088 508	4 056 126	4 781 071
Trade creditors	3 761 913	3 761 913	2 650 291	2 650 291
Other creditors	1 600 072	2 326 595	1 405 835	2 130 780
Regularization accounts	5 984	5 984	6 958	6 958
Accruals and deferred				
income	5 984	5 984	6 958	6 958
Difference on exchange	505 736	505 736	707 664	707 664
TOTAL	29 282 628	29 282 628	26 952 030	26 952 030

EXTRACT 4.   **TYPICAL US BALANCE SHEET**

Balance sheet of GE at 31 December 1988

	General Electric Company and consolidated affiliates	
At December 31 (In millions)	1988	1987
Assets		
Cash	$ 2,187	$ 2,543
Marketable securities carried at cost	5,779	5,353
Marketable securities carried at market	5,089	4,000
Securities purchased under agreements to resell	13,811	12,889
Current receivables	6,780	6,745
Inventories	6,486	6,265
GEFS financing receivables (investment in time sales, loans and financing leases) – net	35,832	27,839
Other GEFS receivables	4,699	4,458
Property, plant and equipment (including equipment leased to others) – net	13,611	12,973
Investment in GEFS	–	–
Intangible assets	8,552	5,748
All other assets	8,039	6,601
Total assets	$110,865	$ 95,414
Liabilities and equity		
Short-term borrowings	$ 30,422	$ 23,873
Accounts payable	6,004	5,728
Securities sold under agreements to repurchase	13,864	13,187
Securities sold but not yet purchased, at market	2,088	1,407
Progress collections and price adjustments accrued	3,504	3,760
Dividends payable	369	319
All other GE current costs and expenses accrued	5,549	4,867
Long-term borrowings	15,082	12,517
Reserves of insurance affiliates	4,177	3,549
All other liabilities	6,986	6,325
Deferred income taxes	3,373	3,100
Total liabilities	91,418	78,632
Minority interest in equity of consolidated affiliates	981	302
Common stock (926,564,000 shares issued)	584	584
Other capital	823	878
Retained earnings	17,950	15,878
Less common stock held in treasury	(891)	(860)
Total share owners' equity	18,466	6,480
Total liabilities and equity	$110,865	$ 95,414

EXTRACT 5.   **INCOME STATEMENT: VERTICAL BY STAGE OF PRODUCTION**

Consolidated statement of income of the Akzo Group, 1989

Millions of guilders		1989		1988
Net sales		18,736.2		16,580.5
Cost of sales		(12,068.6)		(10,682.6)
Gross margin		6,667.6		5,897.9
Selling expenses	(3,135.3)		(2,875.7)	
Research and development expenses	(903.5)		(809.8)	
General and administrative expenses	(963.3)		(821.0)	
Other revenue from operations	47.2		32.8	
		(4,954.9)		(4,473.7)
Operating income		1,712.7		1,424.2
Financing charges		(323.8)		(254.8)
Operating income less financing charges		1,388.9		1,169.4
Taxes		(507.1)		(409.2)
Earnings of consolidated companies from normal operations, after taxes		881.8		760.2
Earnings from nonconsolidated companies		85.8		123.3
Group income from normal operations, after taxes		967.6		883.5
Extraordinary items after taxes		12.2		(11.3)
Group income		979.8		872.2
Minority interest		(25.6)		(29.5)
Net income		954.2		842.7

In The Netherlands, this has also been the tradition; the words *getrouw beeld* (faithful picture) appear in a 1970 law.

In the US and Canada, the requirement is to present fairly, which is a similar concept. 'Substance over form' is a related idea, of considerable significance in the English-speaking world. For example, finance leases are capitalised in the US and the UK because this is thought to reflect commercial substance rather than superficial legal form.

In EC member states (except the three mentioned above) and in Japan, taxation rules, rigid laws and secrecy have been dominant forces in

EXTRACT 6.   **INCOME STATEMENT: VERTICAL BY NATURE OF EXPENSE**

Statement of income of the MAN Group, 1988–1989

	1988–89 TDM 000s	1987–88 TDM 000s
Sales	17,053,699	14,962,096
Changes in inventories, and other own work capitalized	292,265	− 28,949
Total operating performance	17,345,964	14,933,147
Other operating income	382,196	414,773
Cost of materials	− 10,630,182	− 8,748,306
Personnel costs	− 4,177,167	− 4,079,905
Depreciation	− 534,760	− 518,968
Other operating expenses	− 1,921,798	− 1,753,783
Income from shareholdings	53,930	50,860
Write-down of financial assets and securities held as current assets	− 20,789	− 12,816
Income from interest	32,016	56,509
Income from ordinary activities	529,410	341,511
Taxes on income	− 275,783	− 139,792
Consolidated net income	253,627	201,719
Profit brought forward from the previous year	79	111
Minority interest in profit	− 17,263	− 24,939
Minority portion of losses	1,442	1,766
Transfer to retained earnings	− 129,888	− 90,887
Unappropriated profit	107,997	87,770

accounting. This means that depreciation, bad debt provisions and some asset valuations are strongly influenced by tax rules, as illustrated in Chapter III.

The EC Fourth Directive requires the true and fair view to predominate. This has had differing effects. In France, the 1983 Companies Act requires *une image fidèle*. In individual company accounts this is largely catered for by extra disclosures of tax effects and so on. However, in consolidated accounts the effects are more obvious: the capitalisation of leases; a move away from tax valuations (with the consequent appearance of deferred tax); less use of vague provisions (see the next section); adoption of user-friendly formats; and far greater disclosures.

By contrast, in Germany the 1985 Act appears to break the Directive by not requiring the true and fair view to override other provisions of the law (the translation is 'ein den tatsächlichen Verhältnissen entsprechendes Bild'). Further, tax valuations are not departed from even in consolidated accounts; they are merely to be disclosed where material.

Provisions

An initial problem to address is that the words 'provision' and 'reserve' are used rather loosely. In English, this is the case in North America, where a provision for bad debts may be called an allowance or a reserve. For continental European accounts, after translation into American or British English, the subtleties of these words are frequently lost.

In the UK, a provision is an expense. It is, in a sense, an anticipation of a future expense or loss which is at present uncertain in size or probability. However, it relates to a past event: a bad debt provision relates to a past sale; a depreciation provision to past wearing out; a provision for a lawsuit to past unfair dismissals; and so on. The provision leads to a charge against profit and to the setting up of a provision account, which is a liability account or a reduction in an asset account.

By contrast, a reserve is merely an allocation of the profit that has already been calculated. The reserve will often indicate that profits must not be depreciated or that the directors intend not to distribute the profits.

Consequently, the distinction between provisions and reserves is of great importance. The setting up of a £1 million provision has the effects of lowering earnings by £1 million and raising liabilities (lowering net assets) by £1 million. The setting up of a £1 million reserve has no effect on any aggregates or ratios that analysts think important.

Income smoothing

The influences which lead to a proliferation of significant provisions appear to be conservatism and rigid but generous tax regulations. Both these factors are discussed later in this chapter, and their effects on provisions mentioned. The result of such provision accounting may be that the accruals convention and 'fairness' are partially overridden; this in turn may result in income smoothing. The use of accelerated depreciation in the financial accounts is an example of over-provision. The lack of provision for bad debts merely because it is not allowed for tax purposes is an example of under-provision. Provisions for risks and contingencies which fluctuate in reverse relationship with profits are examples of income smoothing. This will be illustrated using several different years of the annual reports of French and German companies.

In the 1983 Annual Report of CFP, a French company, there is a Chartered Accountants' Report (p. A5) which notes that in the UK 'the provision

EXTRACT 7. EXAMPLE OF ACCOUNTS LACKING SHAREHOLDER ORIENTATION

Balance sheet of Fiat at 31 December 1987 (Lire)

Assets	Balance at December 31, 1987	Balance at December 31, 1986	Increase/ (Decrease)
Long-term Investments			
Investments			
Subsidiary companies	5,976,175,253,484	4,111,429,260,623	1,864,745,992,861
Associated companies	7,103,845,428	1,737,319,796	5,366,525,632
Other companies and joint ventures	1,019,057,039	912,057,039	107,000,000
Fixed-income securities	5,984,298,155,951	4,114,078,637,458	1,870,219,518,493
	141,285,443	144,408,193	(3,122,750)
Loans			
Subsidiary companies	41,162,633,000	1,611,916,897,473	(1,570,754,264,473)
Total long-term investments	6,025,602,074,394	5,726,139,943,124	299,462,131,270
Other Long-term Assets			
Property, plant and equipment			
Non-industrial land and buildings	185,971,212	185,971,212	–
Industrial land and buildings	95,658,168,436	97,088,753,275	(1,430,584,839)
Plant and equipment	21,040,318,874	21,036,002,733	4,316,141
Furniture and fittings	8,385,054,950	6,092,907,723	2,292,147,227
Motor vehicles	40,702,686,086	38,795,776,346	1,906,909,740
	165,972,199,558	163,199,411,289	2,772,788,269
Intangibles			
Trademarks	243,978,562	203,707,646	40,270,916
Total other long-term assets	166,216,178,120	163,403,118,935	2,813,059,185
Receivables and Liquid Assets			
Short-term loans and advances			
Subsidiary companies	3,777,377,166,626	2,718,198,992,984	1,059,178,173,642
Associated companies	466,956,674	–	466,956,674
Other companies and joint ventures	260,505,437,983	132,139,268,302	128,366,169,681
	4,038,349,561,283	2,850,338,261,286	1,188,011,299,997

Cash and marketable securities			
Cash at banks	659,427,236,716	611,113,000,551	48,314,236,165
Fixed-income securities	1,022,884,594,994	988,324,953,256	34,559,641,738
Cash on hand	693,385,842	771,011,000	(77,625,158)
	1,683,005,217,552	1,600,208,964,807	82,796,252,745
Accounts receivable maturing within one year			
Third parties	4,251,401,326	5,702,124,052	(1,450,722,726)
Subsidiary companies	12,622,309,224	10,115,378,168	2,506,931,056
Associated companies	4,577,509	2,901,000	1,676,509
Other companies and joint ventures	1,019,280,893	1,100,159,516	(80,878,623)
	17,897,568,952	16,920,562,736	977,006,216
Advances to suppliers			
Third parties	82,500,000	1,291,618,220	(1,209,118,220)
Subsidiary companies	355,655,200	237,186,360	118,468,840
Associated companies	93,894,956	36,873,808	57,021,148
Other receivables	532,050,156	1,565,678,388	(1,033,628,232)
	477,873,528,036	73,398,964,493	404,474,563,543
Total receivables and liquid assets	6,217,657,925,979	4,542,432,431,710	1,675,225,494,269
Accrued Income, Prepaid Expenses and Deferred Charges			
Accrued income	31,037,320,374	32,390,523,840	(1,353,203,466)
Prepaid expenses	1,419,849,260	1,353,086,517	66,762,743
Deferred charges, net	11,800,176,874	14,857,650,743	(3,057,473,869)
Total accrued income, prepaid expenses and deferred charges	44,257,346,508	48,601,261,100	(4,343,914,592)
Total assets	12,453,733,525,001	10,480,576,754,869	1,973,156,770,132
Memorandum Accounts			
Assets belonging to third parties	473,254,452,442	314,200,367,883	159,054,084,559
Company assets with third parties	1,035,178,972,473	1,479,721,433,086	(444,542,460,613)
Commitments	3,413,351,403	39,068,805,475	(35,655,454,072)
Special risks and guarantees	2,036,123,704,401	1,466,740,495,808	569,383,208,593

	Balance at December 31, 1987	Balance at December 31, 1986	Increase/(decrease)
Income items subject to deferred tax deductibility	68,895,853,042	88,539,861,210	(19,644,008,168)
Total memorandum accounts	3,616,866,333,761	3,388,270,963,462	228,595,370,299
Grand Total	16,070,599,858,762	13,868,847,718,331	2,201,752,140,431

Liabilities

	Balance at December 31, 1987	Balance at December 31, 1986	Increase/(decrease)
Capital Stock and Equity Reserves			
Capital stock			
1,404,000,000 ordinary shares	1,404,000,000,000	1,350,000,000,000	54,000,000,000
630,943,000 preference shares	630,943,000,000	664,055,905,000	(33,112,905,000)
305,057,000 savings shares	305,057,000,000	235,944,095,000	69,112,905,000
Legal reserve	2,340,000,000,000	2,250,000,000,000	90,000,000,000
Extraordinary reserve	468,000,000,000	450,000,000,000	18,000,000,000
Additional paid-in capital	220,526,568,796	150,000,000,000	70,526,568,796
Dividend adjustment reserve	1,117,108,838,125	1,117,108,838,125	–
Special reserve – Law No. 170 of March 18, 1965 and subsequent provisions	54,000,000,000	54,000,000,000	–
Reserve – Art. 34 of Law No. 576 of Dec. 2, 1975	9,777,637,426	9,777,637,426	–
Grants received – Art. 102 of D.P.R. No. 1523 of June 30, 1967	1,695,683,837,907	1,804,210,406,703	(108,526,568,796)
Reserve – Art. 55 of D.P.R. No. 597 of Sept. 29, 1973 (Art. 18 of Law No. 675 of Aug. 12, 1977)	34,258,615,537	34,258,615,537	–
	3,707,810,823	3,707,810,823	–
Dividend equalization account and undistributed retained earnings brought forward	161,811,788,175	153,541,551,860	8,270,236,315
Total capital stock and equity reserves	6,104,875,096,789	6,026,604,860,474	78,270,236,315

Other Reserves

Accumulated depreciation of property, plant and equipment			
Non-industrial land and buildings	144,144,634	139,022,631	5,122,003
Industrial land and buildings	23,466,807,552	21,057,720,330	2,409,087,222
Plant and equipment	16,701,782,797	15,194,187,038	1,507,595,759
Furniture and fittings	4,087,939,262	3,158,047,515	929,891,747
Motor vehicles	21,362,035,067	18,109,970,402	3,252,064,665
	65,762,709,312	57,658,947,916	8,103,761,396
Reserve for doubtful receivables	9,517,686,845	9,757,100,080	(239,413,235)
Reserve for employee severance indemnities	129,197,726,645	129,699,136,199	(501,409,554)
Reserve for income taxes	360,946,619,000	28,184,733,000	332,761,886,000
Reserve for general risks and future charges	23,983,081,402	23,983,081,402	–
Total other reserves	589,407,823,204	249,282,998,597	340,124,824,607

Loans and Payables

Debenture loans			
floating rate issue 1981–1988	–	100,000,000,000	(100,000,000,000)
Loans from banks and other financial institutions, medium and long term			
secured	893,700,000	101,988,340,000	(101,094,640,000)
unsecured	88,679,819,517	29,241,729,497	59,438,090,020
	89,573,519,517	131,230,069,497	(41,656,549,980)
Other loans and advances			
Subsidiary companies	4,725,781,773,232	3,197,238,871,917	1,528,542,901,315
Associated companies	34,174,796	625,000,000	(590,825,204)
Other companies and joint ventures	5,530,539,152	13,653,871,521	(8,123,332,369)
	4,731,346,487,180	3,211,517,743,438	1,519,828,743,742
Accounts payable maturing within one year			
Outside suppliers	8,906,840,814	8,545,645,748	361,195,066
Subsidiary companies	24,719,577,091	20,035,011,401	4,684,565,690
Associated companies	153,235,359	153,235,359	–
Other companies and joint ventures	1,823,217,191	607,996,709	1,215,220,482
	35,602,870,455	29,341,889,217	6,260,081,238

Other payables			
Third parties	88,021,374,923	112,307,430,218	(24,286,055,295)
Associated companies	1,150,000,000	–	1,150,000,000
Joint ventures	4,200,000	–	4,200,000
	89,175,574,923	112,307,430,218	(23,131,855,295)
Total loans and payables	4,945,698,452,075	3,584,397,132,370	1,361,301,319,705
Accrued Expenses and Deferred Income			
Accrued expenses	8,549,920,982	8,524,201,238	25,719,744
Deferred income	4,445,072	10,373,241	(5,928,169)
Total accrued expenses and deferred income	8,554,366,054	8,534,574,479	19,791,575
Net income for the year	805,197,786,879	611,757,188,949	193,440,597,930
Total liabilities, capital stock and reserves	12,453,733,525,001	10,480,576,754,869	1,973,156,770,132
Memorandum Accounts			
Assets belonging to third parties	473,254,452,442	314,200,367,883	159,054,084,559
Company assets with third parties	1,035,178,972,473	1,479,721,433,086	(444,542,460,613)
Commitments	3,413,351,403	39,068,805,475	(35,655,454,072)
Special risks and guarantees	2,036,123,704,401	1,466,740,495,808	569,383,208,593
Income items subject to deferred tax deductibility	68,895,853,042	88,539,861,210	(19,644,008,168)
Total memorandum accounts	3,616,866,333,761	3,388,270,963,462	228,595,370,299
Grand Total	16,070,599,858,762	13,868,847,718,331	2,201,752,140,431

for contingencies would be classified as a reserve'. In earlier years, there were even more revealing remarks in the versions of the annual reports of CFP that were specially prepared for UK readers:

Depreciation of property, plant and equipment was F 2274 million vs F 2283 million in 1976. Provision amounts were lower in 1977 than in 1976, especially because cash flow reflected on the French market did not allow constitution of a provision for foreign exchange fluctuations at the same level as in 1976. (1977, p. 22)

Taking into account these items, income for the year was F 111 million, to which must be added a deduction of F 90 million from the provision for contingencies. Income finally amounts to F 201 million . . . but includes lower exceptional income. (1977, p. 23)

EXTRACT 8.   CONSOLIDATED STATEMENT OF INCOME OF THE AEG GROUP FOR 1 JANUARY TO 31 DECEMBER 1987

	1987		1986	
	Million DM	Million DM	Million DM	Million DM
Sales	11,660		11,220	
Change in inventories and own work capitalized	+ 276		+ 137	
Total Operating Performance		11,936		11,357
Other operating income	+ 533		+ 464	
Cost of materials	− 5,376		− 5,212	
Personnel expenses	− 4,642		− 4,489	
Depreciation of intangible and fixed assets	− 357		− 295	
Other operating expenses	− 2,050		− 1,760	
Investment results (net)	+ 16		+ 2	
Interest income (net)	+ 26		+ 1	
Result from other financial investments and current assets securities (net)	− 3		−	
		− 11,853		− 11,289
Results from Ordinary Business Activity		+ 83		+ 68
Extraordinary results	− 19		−	
Taxes on income	− 16		− 25	
Other taxes	− 48		− 43	
		− 83		− 68
Net Income		−		−
Withdrawals from transfers to revenue reserves	+ 5		− 12	
Minority interest in income and losses	− 5		+ 12	
Group Result		−		−

Following the usual effect of amounts set aside to or written back from depreciation and provisions and an allocation of F 800 million to reconstitute the provision for contingencies, net income for the year totalled F 971 million. (1979, p. 23)

As a result of the 1983 Law requiring fairness, CFP transferred its contingency 'provision' to 'reserves' in 1984. However, not all large French companies have followed this practice.

Turning to Germany, and using AEG as an example, the 1987 profit and loss account illustrated (Extract 8) shows a 'net income' of exactly zero for 1986 and 1987. The inevitable conclusion must be that the income statement is calculated by working backwards from the 'net income' of zero. This is income smoothing on a heroic scale. In 1988, a profit was shown after several years of zero income. However, how reliable is this in Anglo-American terms?

It appears that, in Italy and Spain, the Commercial Codes (which would certainly allow greater use of the accruals convention) have been over-ridden to a large extent by the need to satisfy the requirements of tax inspectors. Only recently, and particularly in Italy, have tax reforms and stronger accounting principles allowed the use of 'fairer' provisions of various types.

Tax-based reserves

There are also tax-based reserves, which are treated as provisions. In order to gain advantage of some tax law, a company must charge income with non-commercial 'expenses'. The following examples of tax-based provisions are quotations taken from the accounts of two German concerns, the first VEBA and the second Henkel:

(27) Other operating expenses These expenses include additions to reserves subject to future taxation of DM 14.4 million, compared to DM 4.4 million in the previous year.

The provision in the consolidated financial statements also includes corresponding amounts from the statements of other German companies, deferred tax liabilities of foreign companies, profits taxes on consolidation adjustments which will be subject to tax at a later date, and the tax portion of special accounts and tax-allowable valuation adjustments still permitted under company law.

Recently it has been possible in some countries to retain the advantage of tax-based provisions in company accounts, yet to move away from the accounting effects of this in consolidated accounts. In France, for example, although not all groups take advantage of this greater separation of tax from financial statements, it is normal for large listed companies. It is not normal for Germany.

A further example of untaxed reserves may be useful. It is in Scandinavian countries that some of the greatest tax effects can be seen, so Sweden is taken as an illustration. Electrolux and Volvo, since they are registered with the SEC in the United States, have to provide a reconciliation with US generally accepted accounting principles. The reconciliations shown here (Extracts 9 and 10) include notes on untaxed reserves. We will use examples like these later to discuss shareholders' equity and net assets (see Chapter VI).

Conservatism

Another traditional adversary of fairness is conservatism. Perhaps because of the different mix of users in different countries, conservatism is of differing strength. For example, the importance of banks in Germany may be a reason for greater conservatism in reporting. It is widely held that bankers are more interested in 'rock-bottom' figures in order to satisfy themselves that long-term loans are safe. At the same time, the consequent lack of those interested in a 'fair' view reduces the importance of the accruals convention which would normally modify conservatism.

In the UK it is now more usual to refer to the concept of 'prudence' (as in SSAP 2 and, now, company law). In many cases, accounting standards are the compromise treaties which settle a battle between conservatism and the accruals concept. For example, it is not fully conservative to allow the capitalisation of any development expenditure as in SSAP 13, but it may be reasonably prudent under certain conditions. A similar argument applies to the taking of profit on long-term contracts as in SSAP 9.

Continental European conservatism is of a more stringent variety, as may be seen from examples in this section. It may be noted that many investment analysts greatly increase a German company's profit figure by a series of adjustments before comparing it with a UK figure (see occasional papers on earnings per share by the Deutsche Vereinigung für Finanzanalyse und Anlageberatung (DVFA)). However, matters have 'improved' somewhat since the Aktiengesetz. Before that, it was suggested that: 'If the nonexistence of a contingency cannot be absolutely determined, then in the interest of protecting the creditor, it must be assumed that such a contingency exists.'[1]

A further example of the protection of creditors is the use of statutory or legal reserves in most continental countries. These are undistributable reserves that are set up out of declared profits. They are an extra protec-

---

[1] J. Semler, 'The German accountant's approach to safeguarding investors' and creditors' interests', *Australian Accountant*, September 1964.

EXTRACT 9.   **FROM ELECTROLUX'S RECONCILIATION TO US GAAP**

The consolidated accounts have been prepared in accordance with Swedish accounting practice, which differs in certain significant respects from American accounting principles (US GAAP). The most important differences are described below:

Write-ups on assets

In certain situations, Swedish practice permits write-ups of fixed assets in excess of acquisition cost. This does not normally accord with US GAAP.

Untaxed reserves

Fiscal legislation in Sweden and some other countries permits allocations to untaxed reserves in order to defer tax payments. Changes in untaxed reserves are reported in the income statement under 'Allocations' and thus affect net income. US GAAP do not permit deduction of such allocations from income.

Adjustment for corporate acquisitions

In accordance with Swedish practice, the Group has earlier booked negative goodwill as a deferred credit, which was taken into income over a maximum of ten years. According to US GAAP, negative goodwill should be deducted from the value of acquired fixed assets and reported as income over the useful lives of these assets.

In accordance with Swedish practice, the tax benefit arising from application of tax-loss carry-overs in acquired companies is deducted by the Group from the current year's tax expense. According to US GAAP, this tax benefit should be booked as a retroactive adjustment of the value of acquired assets.

Deferred taxes

Accounts and income taxes are affected during different periods by certain items. Swedish accounting principles do not require reporting of the effect on taxes that is generated by differences in timing. US GAAP require that these effects be reported for all significant differences.

Earnings per share

Earnings per share in accordance with Swedish practice are computed on the basis of income after financial items. US GAAP require that earnings per share be computed on the basis of consolidated net income for the year.

Application of US GAAP would have the following approximate effects on consolidated net income, shareholders' equity and the balance sheet:

A. Consolidated net income

	1988 SEKm	1987 SEKm
Net income as reported in the income statement	1,693	1,282
Depreciation on write-ups of fixed assets	16	10
Allocations	969	844
Adjustment for corporate acquisitions	− 196	71
Deferred taxes	− 377	− 378
Other	− 5	–
Interest on convertible loans after tax	3	4
Adjusted approximate consolidated net income according to US GAAP, fully diluted	2,103	1,833
Approximate net earnings per share, according to US GAAP, fully diluted (SEK) (73,437,198 and 73,451,383 shares)	28.60	25.00

B. Shareholders' equity

	1988 SEKm	1987 SEKm
Shareholders' equity as reported in the balance sheet	11,440	9,914
Items which augment equity		
Untaxed reserves	5,059	4,231
Accelerated depreciation on goodwill	–	275
	5,059	4,506
Items which diminish equity		
Write-ups on fixed assets	– 277	– 281
Adjustment for corporate acquisitions	– 928	– 562
Deferred taxes		
On untaxed reserves	– 2,529	– 2,115
On other items	42	– 122
	– 3,692	– 3,080
Net increase in equity	1,367	1,426
Approximate shareholders' equity according to US GAAP	12,807	11,340

C. Balance sheet

The table below summarizes the consolidated balance sheets prepared in accordance with Swedish accounting principles and US GAAP.2

	According to Swedish principles		According to US GAAP	
	1988 SEKm	1987 SEKm	1988 SEKm	1987 SEKm
Current assets	34,245	31,182	35,810	32,229
Real estate, machinery and equipment	15,722	13,282	15,161	12,659
Shares and participations	2,301	427	2,301	427
Long-term receivables	557	618	557	618
Goodwill	3,287	2,440	2,850	2,715
Other assets	728	521	728	521
Total assets	56,840	48,470	57,407	49,169
Current liabilities	24,597	18,869	26,162	19,916
Long-term liabilities	15,069	14,759	15,069	14,759
Deferred taxes	611	637	3,126	2,896
Untaxed reserves	4,905	4,054	–	–
Minority interests	218	237	243	258
Shareholders' equity	11,440	9,914	12,807	11,340
Total liabilities and shareholders' equity	56,840	48,470	57,407	49,169

tion for creditors above the normal Anglo-American maintenance of capital rules. In France, Germany, Belgium and Italy a company is required to appropriate 5% tranches of its annual profit until the statutory reserve reaches 10% of issued share capital (20% in Italy).

Tangible fixed assets

It is easier to put a reliable value on tangible fixed assets (such as land, buildings and machines) than on intangibles (such as patents, licences and trade marks). Nevertheless, there are still many ways in which valuation can be done, and predominant practice differs country by country across the world.

Historical cost is the traditional method of asset valuation in most countries. Some European countries are looked at in more detail below, as we have already examined the UK and the US.

Germany and Belgium
These countries practise strict historical cost, except for write-downs for depreciation and other tax-allowed reductions. This latter point applies to most countries and will not be repeated.

France
Historical cost is used, except that assets were revalued in 1978 at 1976 values in a tax-exempt way, subsequent depreciation being based on these values. For group accounts, valuations can move away from these tax-controlled numbers. The following example is taken from the accounts of Total Oil for 1987:

Fixed assets – 1976 revaluation
Gross fixed assets of the French companies are included in the consolidated balance sheet at their book values. Fixed assets revalued by these companies in 1978 are accordingly included at their revised value.

In order to ensure consistency in the revaluation of Group assets, revaluations carried out by the foreign subsidiaries (but not incorporated in their own accounts), which are based upon the methods used by the French companies, have been included in the consolidated balance sheet.

Italy, Greece and Spain
These countries are somewhat similar to France, with tax-induced revaluations in the 1980s.

EXTRACT 10.   **FROM VOLVO'S RECONCILIATION TO US GAAP (SEK MILLION)**

Net Income

	1986	1985
Net income as reported in the Consolidated Statements of Income (in accordance with Swedish accounting principles)	2,551	2,546
Items increasing (decreasing) reported income:		
Allocations to untaxed reserves (Note A)	2,694	3,330
Income taxes	(1,547)	(1,975)
Tooling costs	110	323
Equity method investments	113	122
Write-down of investments	(500)	–
Business combinations	80	192
Foreign currency translation	(530)	(808)
Other	(15)	4
Net increase in income before extraordinary income	405	1,188
Income before extraordinary income	2,956	3,734
Extraordinary income	–	744
Approximate net income in accordance with US GAAP	2,956	4,478
Per share amounts, SEK:		
Income before extraordinary income	38.10	48.10
Extraordinary income	–	9.60
Approximate net income per share in accordance with US GAAP	38.10	57.70
Weighted average number of shares outstanding (in thousands)	77,605	77,605

Shareholders' equity

	1986	1985
Shareholders' equity as reported in the Consolidated Balance Sheets (in accordance with Swedish accounting principles)	10,124	8,798
Items increasing (decreasing) reported shareholders' equity:		
Untaxed reserves (Note A)	20,980	17,738
Income taxes	(11,950)	(10,279)
Tooling costs	1,269	1,159
Equity method investments	(233)	211
Business combinations	(282)	35
Other	184	142
Net increase in reported shareholders' equity	9,968	9,006
Approximate shareholders' equity in accordance with US GAAP	20,092	17,804

Note A. Allocations to untaxed reserves

Tax legislation in Sweden and certain other countries permits companies to make allocations to untaxed reserves, which are used principally to strengthen a company's financial position through the deferral of income taxes. To qualify as a tax deduction, Swedish tax law requires that these allocations must be deducted for financial reporting purposes. In accordance with US GAAP, such allocations are not recognized as a reduction of income for financial reporting purposes.

Switzerland

Historical cost applies, except that consolidated accounts are not compulsory so that no valuation rules apply. For example, Ciba-Geigy have been using current cost in their group accounts:

In the Summary of Financial Results, both sales on the one hand and expenses and costs on the other are stated at current value. Depreciation at current value assists in the maintenance of physical capital, and the appearance of paper profits in the accounts is avoided.

The current value principle is applied to the Summary of Financial Status by means of adjustments to the fixed assets and revaluation of stocks.

Sweden

Historical cost is used in Sweden.

The Netherlands

Practice here is somewhat like that in the UK, except that some companies use replacement cost as the main basis of valuation, as shown in the following extract from the accounts for Heineken in 1989:

Accounting policies for the valuation of assets and liabilities.
Fixed assets Tangible fixed assets have been valued on the basis of replacement cost and, with the exception of sites, after deduction of cumulative depreciation. The replacement cost is based on valuations by internal and external experts, taking technical and economic developments into account. They are supported by the experience gained in the construction of establishments all over the world.

However, this is by no means majority Dutch practice and it has become less common since the 1970s.

Denmark

Danish practice is somewhat like that in the UK. Revaluations are fairly common, as in this example from ISS for 1989:

Fixed assets Fixed assets other than land and certain buildings are stated at historical cost prices. Land and buildings held in Denmark were revalued in 1986 to market value in accordance with a public valuation. Development expenditure where appropriate is capitalised.

Disclosure of tax-based valuations

The Fourth Directive requires the disclosure of valuations that are determined by tax rules rather than by commercial or company law provisions. It is becoming increasingly easy to detect major instances of this, as the following German example of Henkel shows:

> In the financial statements of Henkel KGaA at December 31, 1987, all differences between valuations allowable under company law regulations and valuations made solely in accordance with tax regulations are shown as special accounts with a reserve element. In the consolidated financial statements these special accounts are added to revenue reserves, after allowing for deferred taxation at the average rate chargeable on profits of the Group.

Investment properties

A particular quirk of the UK and Ireland, as has been mentioned, is that the relevant accounting standard (SSAP 19) requires investment properties to be annually revalued and not to be subject to systematic depreciation. In other countries investment properties are not treated differently from other properties.

Intangible assets

Practice in this area varies greatly from country to country, and within a country. Goodwill on consolidation is a particular problem which is left for later.

For example, in Germany it was normal until the end of 1987 (when the EC Fourth Directive came into force) to write many intangible assets down to zero on purchase, as the following extract from AEG illustrates:

> Under the intangible assets, patents and similar rights acquired in 1987 are valued for the first time at cost, less scheduled amortization [i.e. they were valued at zero before].

This is still possible outside the EC. At the other extreme, in the late 1980s, some UK companies began to value and capitalise internally developed brand names. The valuation method appears to be current cost, which is legal.

In general, however, intangible assets are valued, like other fixed assets, at historical cost less depreciation.

Under certain conditions, development expenditure can be capitalised and written off over its useful economic life in some countries (e.g. the UK, France, Sweden, Spain, Denmark and The Netherlands), but it cannot be in others (e.g. the US, Germany). Formation expenses may be capitalised and written off over five years in France, Germany, The Netherlands and Spain, but must not be capitalised in the US, the UK, Denmark and Ireland.

Stocks (Inventories)

The 'lower of cost and market' rule is used throughout most of the world, as a means of ensuring the prudent valuation of stock. It is required by the EC Fourth Directive. In most countries 'market' means net realisable value, but it can mean other valuations; for example, in the US it usually means replacement cost. In Germany and Spain, replacement cost would be used where this is even lower than historical cost or net realisable value, as shown in the following example for Union Explosivos of Spain:

> Stocks are valued at cost which is less than replacement cost or net realizable value. The criteria used in establishing cost are as follows:
> Materials and supplies:
>   At purchase cost calculated on a first-in, first-out basis.
> Work-in-progress and finished goods:
>   At manufactured cost calculated on a first-in, first-out basis, including materials and supplies, direct and indirect labour costs, depreciation and other related manufacturing charges.

In The Netherlands some companies value at the lower of replacement cost and net realisable value.

The determination of cost may involve the use of FIFO (first in, first out), LIFO (last in, first out), weighted average or some other method. In the UK, Ireland, France and Sweden, LIFO is not allowed for tax or accounting purposes. In Germany and Spain, LIFO is allowed where it corresponds to physical usage. In The Netherlands, LIFO is allowed but unusual. As already noted, in the US it is the predominant method.

The treatment of overheads can vary. In most countries only production overheads are included, but in Germany and Sweden the appropriate proportion of administration overheads may also be included. In Denmark, even production overheads are not always included, as with Novo Nordisk for 1989:

Inventories

Inventories are stated at cost or market, whichever is lower. Cost is determined on the first-in-first-out basis and comprises direct materials and energy but does not include direct labour and production overheads.

Long-term contracts are accounted for on the percentage-of-completion method in the US, the UK, Ireland and The Netherlands; this allows a proportion of profit to be taken as production proceeds. By contrast, the recording of profit usually waits for completion in France, Germany and Sweden.

Debtors

As a result of prudence, debtors are valued in all countries with reference to future expected receipts rather than to legal obligations outstanding. Specific and general provisions for doubtful debts are deducted from debtors and charged as expenses. For countries within the EC, the Fourth Directive requires separate disclosure of any amounts included under debtors (and therefore under current assets) that are not expected to be received within a year from the balance sheet date.

In some countries, such as Germany and Italy, there may be a tendency to increase general provisions because these are tax deductible. Also in some countries, such as Italy, conventional individual company accounts show provisions for bad debts as a liability item rather than as a deduction from the asset 'debtors'.

Foreign currency debtors in a company's balance sheet might be shown at either the transaction rate or the balance sheet rate. In the UK, the US, Ireland and The Netherlands the balance sheet rate is used. The transaction rate would be regarded as irrelevant, and the balance sheet rate as the better guess for the future settlement rate.

In Germany and Sweden, foreign currency debtors are often valued at the lower of the amounts that would be calculated under the transaction and balance sheet rates. This is a further example of conservatism. Once again an example is provided by the German company Henkel:

> Accounts receivable and payable in foreign currency are translated in the financial statements of individual companies at the rates of exchange in force when they first originated. If, however, translation of foreign currency items at the rate in force on the balance sheet date produces a lower or higher amount respectively, then foreign currency items are translated at the rates in force on the balance sheet date.

In France, company accounts and tax accounts use transaction rates, but group accounts may use the closing rate.

V. GROUPS

One of the most important areas of international difference in accounting is consolidation. Not only do techniques of consolidation vary from country to country, but the very existence of group accounting is by no means universal.

The spread of consolidation

USA

Most practices seem to have first enjoyed widespread adoption in the USA: for example, the normal acquisition (purchase) method of accounting for a business combination. There are examples of consolidation at least as far back as the 1890s, and it was widespread practice by the early 1920s. The various factors that might have caused this early development in the USA may help to explain the diversity in the EC. The US factors may have been:

- A wave of mergers at the turn of the century, leading to the carrying on of business by groups of companies
- The prevalence of the holding company (which merely owns investments) as opposed to the parent company (which is one of the operating companies of the group)
- The lack of a legal requirement for holding/parent company balance sheets, unlike the UK or German law for example
- The lack of legal or other barriers to the emergence of new techniques and the existence of innovative professionals
- The use of consolidation for tax purposes (1917 to 1934)
- The acceptance of consolidation by the New York Stock Exchange (1919).

UK

In the UK, consolidation came later. Holding companies were perhaps less important until during World War I, although there was a UK wave of mergers at the turn of the century. Nevertheless, UK mergers did not usually involve holding companies. Also, tax never moved to a consolidated basis in the UK. It used to be commonly held that Nobel Industries (ICI) pioneered consolidation in the early 1920s and Dunlop in the 1930s. However, Edwards and Webb[1] have found much earlier evidence.

---

[1] J.R. Edwards and K.M. Webb, 'The development of group accounting in the UK to 1933', *Accounting Historians Journal*, Spring 1984.

The Stock Exchange required consolidation as a condition of new issues from 1939; and consolidation became almost universal after the Companies Act 1948.

Continental Europe

In The Netherlands, consolidation was also practised by the 1930s. However, in most of continental Europe, consolidation is either a recent development or still very rare. In Germany, consolidation was made obligatory by the 1965 Aktiengesetz for public companies. However, foreign subsidiaries did not need to be (and generally were not) consolidated, and the use of the equity method for associated companies was not allowed. Further, there were important differences from Anglo-American practice in the use of an economic (rather than a legal) basis for 'the group', and a yearly calculation of 'differences arising on consolidation' based on book values rather than a once-for-all calculation of goodwill based on fair values. West Germany implemented the Seventh Directive in 1985, thus removing most of these differences from 1990 (see also Chapter VIII).

In France before 1985 there was no law on consolidation, and consolidation had been very rare. However, the formation of COB in the late 1960s and the influence of Anglo-American practices, due to the presence of international firms and the desire of some French companies for listings on the Exchanges of London or New York, caused a gradual increase in consolidation by listed companies. Naturally, in a country where there is no tradition of professional accounting measurement standards, in cases where there were no law or tax requirements the practice has been very varied. The Conseil National de la Comptabilité, a government body with responsibility for the *plan*, issued guidelines in 1968 and 1978. However, these guidelines were not followed exactly. In 1985 a law was passed to require listed companies to publish consolidated financial statements by 1987 year ends. Other companies had to follow by 1989.

In Belgium and Spain, until the 1980s, consolidation was very rare. In Italy, CONSOB has been encouraging consolidation, but it has been rare even for listed companies. The result of lack of consolidation in these many EC countries is that outside investors or lenders (particularly foreigners) have grossly inadequate information, even about large listed groups. The situation in Switzerland is broadly the same. Extracts 11 and 12 show the best available set of accounts for a large Swiss group, Holzstoff. It appears that there are no buildings or machines, and no sales or wages. This is because the best available accounts are those of the holding company, whereas all the operations are performed in subsidiaries. Of course, it is even more confusing when **part** of the group's operations is performed by the parent.

One of the effects of this rarity of consolidation was that the EC's major draft law on financial reporting (the Fourth Directive) was adopted in 1978 without any recognition of group accounting. Presumably, when the first draft was published in 1971, a requirement to consolidate would have been hopelessly controversial.

However, as we have seen, the stock exchange bodies and governments of most EC countries have begun to take action to require listed or public companies to consolidate. This is designed to make their domestic capital markets more efficient and to internationalise the flows of capital. It is of course logical to direct the consolidation rules at those companies where outside providers of finance are important. The Seventh Directive of the EC (adopted in 1983) requires consolidation rules by 1990 (see Chapter VIII).

The scope of the group: control and ownership

The purpose of consolidation is to present the accounts of the group as if it were a single entity. However, the exact scope of the group, and whether to consolidate all of it, are debatable matters. The first question is whether the group is the set of enterprises under common control or the set under common ownership. The logic of group accounting makes it clear that control is what really matters. Consequently, there is no debate that 100% of the assets, income etc. of a subsidiary should be consolidated even if it is only 75% owned. That amount of ownership will allow 100% control. This also makes it clear, for example, that a foreign subsidiary should be excluded from consolidation if the foreign government restricts management or bans distribution of profits. Doubts about control and about international accounting differences led German law to allow the exclusion of all foreign subsidiaries (until 1990 year ends). However, most countries include normal foreign subsidiaries.

For the purposes of illustration, let us use the group in Figure 2. Where there is a sub-subsidiary in which the group owns 36%, this could easily still be controlled (see S11 in the figure). Furthermore, even the 45% holding in S2 could make it a subsidiary if the remaining shares were widely spread and in practice exercised no control. French law imposes a rebuttable presumption that holdings of even 40% imply parentage. Traditional practice in The Netherlands and France has been to stress control as the criterion for consolidation.

In the UK, the USA and Germany, by contrast, although control is seen as the reason for consolidation, ownership is viewed as the most readily auditable proxy for the existence of control. Under the EC's Seventh Directive on company law (discussed also in Chapter VIII) there are six identifiable criteria for consolidation; most of them rest upon ownership. Table 18 shows the UK definitions. Despite these complex rules, in most cases a subsidiary is a company in which the group holds more than half the voting shares.

EXTRACT II.   **BALANCE SHEET OF HOLZSTOFF HOLDING INC. AT 31.12.1986**

SFr.

Assets

Investments	73 523 170.–
Loans to group companies	33 068 800.–
Accounts receivable	2 839 436.34
Securities	3 328 330.–
Cash and cash items	46 399 694.46
Total	159 159 430.80

Liabilities and equity

Share capital	40 000 000.–
Legal reserves	4 840 000.–
Special reserves	22 200 000.–
Debentures 4 1/2, due 1992	15 000 000.–
4 3/4, due 1993	20 000 000.–
Accounts payable	138 476.80
Provisions	48 209 590.–
Retained earnings	282 860.36
Earnings	8 488 503.64
Total	159 159 430.80

EXTRACT 12.   **INCOME STATEMENT OF HOLZSTOFF HOLDING INC. FOR 1986**

SFr.

Revenues

Revenue from investments	12 437 023.13
Interest income	2 967 437.96
Other revenue	388 249.95
Dissolution of the provision for cost of group reorganisation	–
Total	15 792 711.04

Expenditures

Interest expense	1 625 000.–
Taxes	1 646 207.40
Depreciation and provisions	4 033 000.–
Cost of group reorganisation	–
Earnings	8 488 503.64
Total	15 792 711.04

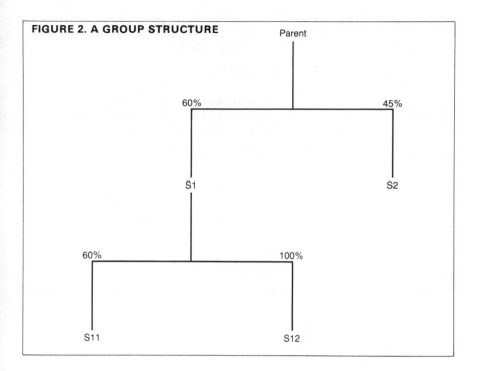

FIGURE 2. A GROUP STRUCTURE

Goodwill is the excess of the cost of an investment in a subsidiary (or associate or joint venture) over the proportion of net assets acquired. It is gradually becoming international practice for the net assets of the subsidiary to be measured at 'fair values' at the acquisition date for this purpose (as an estimate of 'cost' to the group). However, in most continental European countries the traditional method has been to compare the cost of investment with the book value of the group's share of the subsidiary's net assets. This means a larger goodwill figure. The Seventh Directive requires the use of fair values or a method that gives similar results that is now used in Germany (see Example 4 in Chapter I). Nevertheless, the book value method still continues in some EC and some other European countries.

Goodwill

Once goodwill has been calculated, at least three subsequent treatments can be found:

1. Leave the goodwill in the balance sheet at the acquisition level. This is not permissible under the Seventh Directive but is not unknown in Europe.
2. Show the goodwill as an asset but amortise it over its useful life. This is the predominant practice. French and Swedish companies often use ten years, German companies fifteen years.

TABLE 18. DEFINITIONS OF A SUBSIDIARY (UK 1989 ACT BASED ON SEVENTH DIRECTIVE)

Any one of the following will establish a parent/subsidiary relationship: where the parent:

1.	(a)	Has the majority of voting rights; or
	(b)	Has the right to exercise dominant influence over the subsidiary because of a contract or provisions in the memorandum or articles; or
2.		Is a member of the subsidiary and
	(a)	Controls the majority of votes on the board of directors, or
	(b)	Controls by agreement the majority of voting rights; or
3.		Has a participating interest and
	(a)	Exercises dominant influence, or
	(b)	Manages on a unified basis.

---

3. Write the goodwill off immediately against reserves, thereby never showing an asset and never suffering amortisation charges. This is predominant practice in the UK and Ireland, and is common in The Netherlands.

Associates and joint ventures

Some enterprises are not controlled by a group but are, nevertheless, significantly influenced by one. It has gradually become standard international practice to account for investments in such companies by a form of partial consolidation, usually called the equity method or one-line consolidation. Under this method, instead of bringing into the group balance sheet only the cost of the investment, the group's proportion of the equity (or net assets) of the enterprise is accounted for in a single line. In the UK and Ireland, such enterprises are called associates; in the US (and therefore in some continental countries) they are called, for example, 'companies consolidated by the equity method'.

In the group profit and loss account, the equity method involves taking the group's proportion of the net profit and tax of the associate. The normal position for this is 'above the line'; that is, included in earnings. This can be seen in the account shown for the UK company Jaguar (Extract 13); the term 'related companies' was replaced by 'associates' from 1990.

For Denmark, associates can also be found above the line, as seen in the income statement shown for Kryolitselskabet (Extract 14).

However, there can be variation. Some but not all French companies show income from associates near the end of the profit and loss account, as in the Bull statement shown as Extract 15.

The exact definition of an associate can vary, but 'significant influence' is now generally presumed for investments of 20% to 50%. At one point in The Netherlands the threshold was 25% and in France $33\frac{1}{3}$%, but the Seventh Directive is harmonising on 20%. In some countries the equity method was illegal (as in Germany until 1987 year ends) or just not used. However, the Seventh Directive makes it compulsory (for example, in Germany from 1990 year ends). In Sweden, most companies do not use the equity method because of doubts about its legality, despite a statement from the accountancy body (FAR) suggesting that it is acceptable in consolidated accounts. In the case of Volvo, the appropriate adjustment to US GAAP is shown in Chapter IV.

Other European countries outside the EC are likely to follow the lead of the Seventh Directive. However, not all do so at present, as may be seen

---

EXTRACT 13. CONSOLIDATED PROFIT AND LOSS ACCOUNT OF JAGUAR PLC FOR THE YEAR ENDED 31 DECEMBER 1988

	1988
	£m
Turnover	1,075.5
Cost of sales	(945.4)
Gross profit	130.1
Distribution costs	(28.0)
Administrative expenses	(62.7)
Operating profit	39.4
Share of profits of related companies	2.9
Net income from investments	5.2
Profit on ordinary activities before taxation	47.5
Taxation on profit on ordinary activities	(19.1)
Profit on ordinary activities after taxation	28.4
Dividends	(20.1)
Retained profit for the financial year	8.3
Retained by	
Jaguar	(13.5)
Subsidiary companies	20.4
Related companies	1.4
	8.3
Earnings per ordinary share of 25p	15.6p

EXTRACT 14. INCOME STATEMENT OF KRYOLITSELSKABET ØRESUND A/S FOR THE FINANCIAL YEAR 1 JANUARY TO 31 DECEMBER 1988

	1988 Dkr. 1,000
NET TURNOVER	1,463,442
Production costs	1,050,728
GROSS INCOME	412,714
Selling, storage and distribution costs	233,843
Administration costs	96,553
Other operating income	8,124
OPERATING INCOME	90,442
Income from associated companies	64
Income from capital investments	14,501
Other financial income	36,187
Financial expenses	59,095
Profit before extraordinary items and taxes	82,099
Extraordinary income	94,503
Extraordinary expenses	71,626
Partner's share of Dansk Salt I/S	21,319
PROFIT FOR THE YEAR BEFORE TAX	83,657
Corporation tax (Income in 1988)	(12,194)
PROFIT FOR THE YEAR	95,851

---

from the following example from Adia of Switzerland, where associates are not treated by the equity method:

Scope   The consolidated statements include the figures of affiliated companies (which close their books at year end), according to the following criteria:
(a) For companies in the service sector:
   When Adia SA owns over 50%, assets, liabilities, revenues and expenses are taken into account for 100%. The profit attributable to minority interests is deducted from the consolidated net profit under the heading 'Minority Interests'.
   When Adia SA owns 50% or less, the consolidation takes into account the value of the investment and the dividends paid as booked in Adia SA.

(b) For all other Group companies:
Irrespective of the percentage held, only the value of the investment and the dividends paid are treated in the consolidation.

In most countries joint ventures are treated as associates. However, the
long-standing practice of some groups in France and The Netherlands is
to use 'proportional consolidation' whereby the group's proportions of
assets, liabilities, revenues and expenses are taken line-by-line into the
group accounts. A typical note on this for a French company, in this case
Total Oil, is as follows:

Consolidation is however proportional, on the one hand for 'joint
interest' companies in which the holding is less than 50% and in
which operations are shared on the basis of each partner's interest,
and on the other hand for companies controlled jointly on a 50/50
basis by the Group and a single other shareholder.

EXTRACT 15.   CONSOLIDATED STATEMENT OF INCOME OF BULL,
1987 (F thousand)

Revenue:	
Sales	10,412,006
Rental, service and other	7,659,199
Total	18,071,205
Costs and expenses:	
Cost of revenue	(10,545,231)
Research and development	(1,551,539)
Selling, general and administrative	(5,487,076)
Interest expense	(845,118)
Interest income	242,622
Other income – net	314,645
Total	(17,871,697)
Profit before income taxes, extraordinary credit and minority interests	199,508
Provision for income taxes	(1,021,317)
Extraordinary credit – income tax benefits of loss carryforwards	985,645
Minority interests	(8,269)
Share of the results of companies consolidated by the equity method	69,634
Net income	225,201

The Seventh Directive gives member states the option to allow proportional consolidation. This option has been taken, for example, in Germany, France and The Netherlands. However, in the UK the method is only available for unincorporated joint ventures.

In some countries, the equity method is used for the treatment of investments even in the parent company's accounts. This is the case in The Netherlands (for subsidiaries and associates) and in Denmark (for subsidiaries). In the parent's accounts, the income that has not been received as dividends is shown as unrealised, as noted here for Kryolitselskabet Øresund A/S of Denmark:

> Investments in subsidiaries are accounted for in the parent company's accounts on the basis of the companies' net book values and results, in accordance with the equity method, thus eliminating unrealized internal margins. Value increases/Group goodwill relating to company take-overs or purchases of shares in subsidiaries have been written down by their full amount in the year of acquisition in the equity of the Group and the parent company. Dividends from subsidiaries have been entered as receivables, and the portion of the companies' profits which is not distributed as dividend is transferred to the subsidiary company reserve.

Segmental reporting

As with many topics in this area, US practice has led the field. US companies following GAAP produce a large amount of information by line-of-business and geographical segment. The data concern sales and net assets.

The EC Directives require turnover to be split by sector and market. This latter requirement can be found in the laws that have implemented the Directives. In the UK, the practice of most large companies goes further because the Companies Act 1985 requires pre-tax profit to be shown by sector. These practices are also included in the Listing Requirements of the International Stock Exchange in London. Further, in 1990 an accounting standard (SSAP 25) was issued which requires disclosure of turnover, pre-tax profit and capital employed, by both sector and market. This approximates to US practice.

In general, practice in continental Europe does not go beyond that required by the rules implemented as a result of the Directives; and segmental reporting is not standard practice outside the EC.

Currency translation

The Seventh Directive does not include rules relating to foreign currency translation. Consequently, the variety of practice in Europe is even greater for this topic than for other matters connected with consolidation. In the

UK, Ireland and The Netherlands there is no law but there are 'standards' on the subject. However, in France and Germany there is no official guidance. In Sweden, the guidance from the accountancy body follows Anglo-American practice. In countries where there are no rules on consolidation, practice on translation is obviously varied.

Transactions

Discussion here will begin with the treatment of foreign currency items in an individual company's own accounts. In all countries it is normal to translate assets into local currency once and for all. For example, consider a British company that bought on credit a German computer invoiced in Deutschmarks. In the UK accounts, and assuming no forward purchasing or matching, this asset would normally be frozen into pounds sterling at the date of purchase.

The next matter to consider is the resulting debtors or creditors in such cases. In most countries, if outstanding at a year end, these amounts would be translated at year-end exchange rates. Thus, there would usually be gains or losses on settlement and at each year end. However, some German, Swiss and Swedish companies take the conservative approach of recording debts at the lower of the amounts in their own currency at the date of sales and at the year end. This was discussed in Chapter IV.

Long-term liabilities in foreign currencies in an individual company's balance sheet are normally translated at year-end rates.

Losses recognised as a result of the above practices are generally taken immediately into the profit and loss account. However, the treatment of gains is more varied. In the UK gains on both short-term and long-term monetary items are taken to profit, even though the gains are unsettled and unrealised. In The Netherlands, short-term gains are taken but not always long-term gains. In France, gains are not recognised for individual company accounts and for tax, but can be for consolidated accounts, as indicated here by Total Oil:

Monetary assets and liabilities of the French companies denominated in foreign currencies are translated at the exchange rates ruling on 31 December. The resulting gains or losses are dealt with in the profit and loss account. Consequently the exchange difference accounts arising through the application of the French Revised Chart of Accounts are eliminated.

In Germany, such gains are not recognised in individual or in group accounts.

Translation of Foreign Financial Statements: Current and Temporal
  Methods

Companies in most countries use the current rate method for the translation of the accounts of foreign subsidiaries. This involves:

1. Balance sheets translated at year-end rates
2. Profit and loss accounts translated at average rates for the year
3. Differences on translation put to reserves.

In the UK, SSAP 20 allows, and many companies use, the closing rate for
profit and loss accounts.
     There follow five extracts from company accounts illustrating currency
translation. In general, US and continental companies use the average
rate for the profit and loss account, as shown for Switzerland by Adia,
France by Total Oil and Bull, and Germany by AEG. However, the treatment of exchange differences is not always uniform; compare the treatment by Total Oil with the Anglo-Amercian treatment by Bull.

Swiss currency translation: Adia
The accounts of foreign Group companies are translated into Swiss francs
according to the following rules: the profit and loss account items are
translated by applying

- The annual average exchange rates (weighted in accordance with the
  monthly sales in the respective currencies) for sales and all other items
  of the profit and loss account, except the net profit figure
- The actual exchange rates for the net profit of the year if already
  transferred
- The average exchange rates for the month of December for the profit of
  the year if not yet transferred.

The differences arising from using the various exchange rates are
grouped under the heading 'Non-operating income' in the consolidated
profit and loss account. Balance sheet items are translated at the average
exchange rates for the month of December.

French currency translation: Total Oil
Foreign company balance sheets are converted into French francs on the
basis of exchange rates at 31 December 1986. This conversion is applied
to fixed assets as well as to monetary assets and liabilities. Gains or
losses on translation of their balance sheets at the end of the previous
year are dealt with:

- In reserves for that part which relates to non-monetary assets (property, plant and equipment, associated companies and trade investments)
- In the profit and loss account for that part which relates to monetary assets (long- and short-term debt and loans and cash balances) and stocks.

Average exchange rates are used for consolidated profit and loss account items so as to approximate to the figures that would be obtained by converting 1986 transactions on a daily basis. However, 'Net income' and 'Allocations for depreciation and provisions' have been converted, in the same way as balance sheet items, using the rate at 31 December 1986.

French currency translation: Bull
The financial statements of the Group's foreign subsidiaries have been translated into French francs, for consolidation purposes, according to the principles of Statement No. 52 of the Financial Accounting Standards Board of the United States of America. These principles are summarised as follows:

- Assets and liabilities, including accumulated depreciation, are translated at year-end exchange rates.
- Income statement amounts are translated at average monthly rates of exchange.

Gains and losses resulting from translation are accumulated in a separate component of stockholders' equity entitled 'Translation adjustment'. The translation adjustments in 1987 and 1986 are reported on a separate line in the Consolidated Statement of Stockholders' Equity.

German currency translation: AEG
The fixed assets of consolidated foreign affiliates and the book values of the non-consolidated foreign affiliates are translated at the median currency exchange rate in effect at the year end of the year of acquisition. All other assets, liabilities and equity are translated at the median exchange rate in effect at the end of the current year.

   In the statement of income, revenue and expense items are translated at the average exchange rates of the current year. Exceptions are the depreciation of fixed assets and gains and losses on the disposal of fixed and financial assets, which are translated at the rates in effect at acquisition. Foreign affiliates' profits and losses for the year are translated at the median exchange rate in effect at the balance sheet date. The difference arising from translating at the average rate for the year and the rate in effect at year end is included under other operating income or expenses.

Danish currency translation: Novo Nordisk, 1989
Assets and liabilities in foreign currencies are translated into Danish kroner at the rates of exchange ruling at the balance sheet date. Financial statements of foreign subsidiaries are translated using exchange rates ruling at the balance sheet date for assets and liabilities and average exchange rates for income and expense items except for subsidiaries in countries with high inflation. In these cases non-monetary assets, liabilities and stockholders' equity are translated at historic exchange rates and all recorded exchange gains and losses are reflected in the income statement.

The major difference in Europe is in the differential use of the temporal method. This method, which was the standard US method in SFAS 8 from 1975 to 1981, requires the use of exchange rates that are appropriate to the valuation basis of the item to be translated. For example, fixed assets (and depreciation charges on them) and stocks held at historical cost are translated at the appropriate historical rates. Most profit and loss account items can normally be translated at average rates; cash and debtors are translated at year-end rates.

In the UK, SSAP 20 calls for the use of the temporal method for very closely held subsidiaries. In practice its use is very rare. SSAP 20 would call for differences on translation to be taken to the profit and loss account, as SFAS 8 used to require. The temporal method is not used in The Netherlands. In France the closing rate and the temporal method are allowed, although the former is more common. The main exponents of the temporal method now are a number of German-based multinationals. They do not all take translation differences to reserves, as shown in the AEG example. Furthermore, the use of the temporal method is sometimes approximate; for example, some companies use the rates of the year end of acquisition of an asset rather than the day of acquisition (again see the AEG example). Assuming that the Deutschmark is usually strong against currencies of subsidiaries, use of the temporal method will raise fixed asset values compared with use of closing rates of exchange, and depreciation charges will also be higher.

In Denmark the temporal method is sometimes used for hyper-inflationary subsidiaries, as it is by US multinationals; this is illustrated in the Novo Nordisk extract.

VI. DIFFICULTIES IN CALCULATING EARNINGS AND NET ASSETS

Even if all the problems of measurement and valuation discussed in Chapters IV and V could be overcome, there would still be great difficulties in arriving at vital aggregates like 'earnings' and 'net assets'. Much analysis depends on these numbers, or simple derivatives of them. This chapter investigates the problems.

Earnings

In several countries, including the UK and the US, 'earnings' is a technical term for a precisely defined type of profit measure. The UK definition can be found in SSAP 3. Earnings are profits:

- After depreciation, interest and other trading and financial expenses
- After taxation on ordinary activities
- After any minority shares of ordinary group profits
- After preference dividends
- But **before** extraordinary items.

Extraordinary items

Extraordinary items are defined (in SSAP 6) as those that are material in size, are not expected to recur and are outside the ordinary activities of the business.

Listed companies in the US and the UK are required to disclose their earnings per share, from which a price/earnings ratio can be calculated. In most continental European countries there is no standard definition and no requirement to show earnings, although some listed companies volunteer the disclosure.

The definition of 'extraordinary' appears to be fixed in the Fourth Directive as 'otherwise than in the course of the company's ordinary activities'. However, in practice the use of the term varies in Europe for several reasons:

1. The Directive is not in force in some countries, such as (at the time of writing) Italy, Portugal and, of course, Austria, Switzerland, Sweden etc.
2. Some countries add glosses to the definition: e.g. in the UK and Ireland (SSAP 6), extraordinary items must also be material and not expected to recur.

EXTRACT 16. EXTRAORDINARY ITEMS: F.L.S. SMIDTH & CO., DENMARK (DK MILLION)

Note 5: Extraordinary income

Profit on sale of site	144
Profits on sale of shares	50
Profits on sale of tangible assets	24
Other income	16
	234

Note 6: Extraordinary expenses

Extraordinary losses on completed orders	44
Redundancy payments	35
Extraordinary write-offs on stocks and work-in-progress etc.	31
Losses on sale of tangible assets	14
Losses on sale of properties	4
Other expenses	24
	152

Note: the profit before extraordinaries was DK 71 m

3. Exactly what is meant by 'ordinary activities' varies. For example, in the UK the sale of a shop by a stores group would not be thought to be extraordinary, whereas it probably would be by a French stores group. The German and US definitions are even narrower than the UK definition.

The example shown above uses a public company in Denmark, where the Fourth Directive was implemented in 1981. Of the extraordinary expenses shown, only the second appears to fit the UK definition. Of the gains, the sale of tangible assets may well not have been extraordinary by UK standards.

In Greece the nearest analogous term would be translated as 'non-trading', and in Portugal as 'non-operating'.

The important point is that 'earnings' as used in the UK **exclude** extraordinary items. Analysts may well wish to standardise on this but will be frustrated because of the differing definition of 'extraordinary'. It may be necessary to standardise on profit after extraordinary items, because this is immune to the effects of the definition of 'extraordinary'.

A further complication is the use in the UK and Ireland of the term 'exceptional items', as shown overleaf in the Gallaher account. These are amounts which are **not** thought to be outside ordinary activities but are abnormal in size or incidence. In French, both 'extraordinary' and 'excep-

EXTRACT 17.   CONSOLIDATED PROFIT AND LOSS ACCOUNT OF GALLAHER, 1987 (£ MILLION)

Turnover	3,886.7
Cost of sales	(3,214.6)
Gross profit	672.1
Distribution, advertising and selling costs	(392.1)
Administrative expenses	(101.6)
Other operating income	3.0
Trading profit before exceptional items	181.4
Exceptional items	-
Interest	(11.7)
Profit on ordinary activities before taxation	169.7
Tax on profit on ordinary activities	(62.5)
Profit on ordinary activities after taxation	107.2
Minority interests	(0.3)
Profit before extraordinary items	106.9
Extraordinary items	(5.5)
Profit for the financial year	101.4
Dividends paid	(44.4)
Profit retained for the year	57.0
Statement of retained profits	
At the beginning of the year	482.0
Profit retained for the year	57.0
Exchange adjustments on net investment in overseas subsidiaries	(6.1)
At the end of the year	532.9

tional' are translated as *exceptionnel*, which hardly helps international analysis.

In the UK and Ireland, extraordinaries are shown after 'profit on ordinary activities after taxation'. That is, tax is split between the amount charged on ordinary and that on extraordinary profit. The Gallaher account is typical of the UK; the tax on extraordinary items could be shown on the face of the account but would normally be shown in a note.

By contrast, in most other countries, extraordinaries are shown gross of taxation and above the tax charge, as in the Danish and German account examples shown in Extracts 18 and 19. In Germany, for example,

EXTRACT 18. **PROFIT AND LOSS ACCOUNT OF EAST ASIATIC COMPANY, 1989
(DK THOUSAND)**

Net sales	17,737,507
Cost of sales	13,665,948
Gross profit	4,071,559
Share of earnings before tax in associated companies	138,074
	4,209,633
Selling and distribution expenses	2,191,093
Administrative expenses	1,013,177
Amortisation of goodwill	31,658
Other operating expenses	4,153
Other operating income	117,480
	3,122,601
Operating profit	1,087,032
Dividends from associated companies	
Income from other investments	16,028
	16,028
Profit before financing expenses	1,103,060
Financing income	725,607
Financing expenses	928,414
	202,807
Profit on ordinary activities	900,253
Extraordinary income	365,507
Extraordinary expenses	324,665
	40,842
Profit before taxes	941,095
Provision for income taxes	113,730
Share of tax on earnings in associated companies	68,029
	181,759
	759,336
Allocation to surplus reserve	200,000
Profit before minority interests	559,336
Minority interests	120,190
Net profit	439,146

there are several different types of tax; so 'pre-tax' is ambiguous. Consequently, German companies do not always clearly show pre-tax profits; see the Henkel example. It should be noted that pre-tax profits in the UK are **after** some taxes, such as VAT and property rates.

EXTRACT 19. CONSOLIDATED STATEMENT OF INCOME OF THE HENKEL GROUP, 1987 (DM THOUSAND)

		%
Sales	9,255,915	100.0
Cost of sales	5,409,579	58.4
Gross profit	3,846,336	41.6
Selling and distribution costs	− 2,378,617	25.7
Research and development costs	− 277,307	3.0
Administrative expenses	− 592,844	6.4
Other operating income	+ 82,968	0.9
Other operating charges	− 106,455	1.2
Operating result	574,081	6.2
Financial items	− 42,934	− 0.5
Result from ordinary activities	531,147	5.7
Extraordinary items	− 35,874	− 0.4
Taxes on income	− 200,565	− 2.2
Other taxes	− 2,708	-
Profit for the year	292,000	3.1
Allocation to revenue reserves	− 195,887	− 2.1
Minority interests in profits	− 21,424	− 0.2
Minority interests in losses	+ 1,611	-
Consolidated unappropriated profit	76,300	0.8

Pensions

The provision for pension costs can be a very large expense for many companies. It has become standard practice in the UK and the US to base a year's pension on an actuarial assessment of the degree to which the work done in that particular year will give rise to eventual pension payments. That is, the pay-as-you-go basis is not acceptable; under that system, a new company with a pension scheme but no pensioners would appear to have no pension costs.

However, even between the UK and the US, the differences of technical detail can lead to large differences in yearly charges. This is all the more so for differences between the UK and continental Europe. If the rules for pension costs are lax, it becomes possible to charge too much or too little for pensions, and thereby to manipulate profits. For example, in Germany until 1987 year ends, pension costs did not have to be charged. Consequently the Analysts Association (DVFA) always added back pension costs in order to get more comparable numbers within Germany.

Social conventions also affect this, as explained in Chapter I for UK, French and Italian companies (see table 4).

Dividends

In the East Asiatic Company account (see above), no dividends are shown as being paid. This is generally the case in continental Europe. In the UK and Ireland, a provision is made at the end of the year for the dividends proposed by the directors to be paid from the year's profits. This has to be approved by the AGM, but normally this is a formality. Therefore the accruals convention suggests an accrual. In the accounts of a French company (though not necessarily of a group) there are two columns in a balance sheet, showing 'before allocation' (or 'before AGM decisions') and 'after' (see Chapter IV). In the USA, again, no appropriation is made for dividends to be paid in the following year.

Minority interests

In some countries, for example Germany, the minority interests' share of profit is not seen as a charge against earnings. This is because of the entity concept of the group or *Konzern*, which places less stress on the parent company shareholders. In the Henkel account, profits are shown before minorities. For most other countries this is not the case, as in the Danish and UK examples above. In the UK and the USA, minority share of profits is always extracted in the calculation of earnings.

Reserves

The German company Henkel's reserve movements (see above) take place with items that would be included in earnings in the UK. Another German company (AEG; see Chapter IV) includes them in 'Group result'. By contrast, in the UK, reserve movements are clearly separated, or may be relegated to the notes. In France, the two-column approach handles the problem.

Of course, with two-sided profit and loss accounts it is much more difficult to see what is going on. Two-sided accounts are still presented for individual companies in most European countries.

Tax

For different purposes, readers of accounts may want to use pre-tax or post-tax profit numbers. However, the 'earnings' of a company in Anglo-American practice are always **after** corporate income taxation. As mentioned, in some countries, e.g. Germany, there are many different corporate taxes, so that 'pre-tax profit' is an ambiguous expression.

A further complication is deferred tax. This was discussed in some detail in Chapter II, where it was shown that reversible timing differences between tax and accounting depreciation are a cause of deferred taxation. Other causes of reversible timing differences might be inventory valuation methods or instalment sales. In some countries, such as the USA, these differences are fully accounted for. That is, to continue with the example of accelerated tax depreciation, tax charges might be seen as artificially low in early years. Accounting for deferred tax corrects for this, as a result of the accruals convention.

As discussed in Chapter II, the technique for achieving full accounting for deferred tax is to increase (debit) the tax for the year in the income statement to what it would have been without the generous tax rules. The counter-balancing effect is to create a deferred tax account (credit), which one could interpret as a liability to pay more tax in the future. The debit makes earnings look lower; the credit makes liabilities look worse.

As mentioned in Chapter II, in the UK and Ireland many reversible timing differences arise but standard practice is **not** to account fully for deferred tax. The method used is partial allocation, whereby deferred tax is only recognised as a liability when it is expected to be paid within the foreseeable future (normally three years). Some Dutch, Danish and Italian companies also follow this practice. The following extract is from the accounts of the Danish company ISS for 1989:

Corporation tax and deferred tax
Tax on profit of the year includes payable corporation tax and deferred tax. Provision for deferred tax is made using the liability method for taxation deferred in respect of all timing differences between accounting and taxation treatment, except when it is considered that the tax effect of such deferrals will continue for the foreseeable future.

A UK example is taken from the Marks and Spencer accounts for 1988:

Deferred taxation is provided on the liability method, to the extent that it is probable that a liability will crystallise. It is provided on the excess of capital allowances over depreciation in respect of assets leased to third parties and on certain items of income and expenditure included in the profit and loss account in different years from those in which they are assessed for taxation purposes.

However, in most of continental Europe, deferred tax is not a major problem because of the close relationship between tax and accounting figures. Nevertheless, in consolidated accounts, there may be foreign elements of deferred tax. Furthermore, in France for example, consolidated accounts can now be freed from the dominance of tax; and, when values are changed from those in the individual company accounts, deferred tax may arise.

As an example of the differential international effects, Table 19 shows the relation of asset revaluation to deferred tax. In practice, deferred tax usually only arises for this reason in case 5.

Net assets

Analysts will often be interested in arriving at a total of 'net assets', which is usually the same as 'shareholders' funds' (except that minority interests are not usually included in the latter but should probably be included in the former).

Clearly, all the points above in this chapter will affect these totals, but there are further problems relating to exactly which 'liabilities' to deduct in the calculation of net assets. This point was illustrated for France in Chapter IV, where it was seen that some provisions are really reserves, meaning that they should above be included in shareholders' funds and not deducted in the calculation of net assets.

TABLE 19.   **ASSET REVALUATIONS AND DEFERRED TAX**

	System	*Example country*
1.	Not allowed to revalue	US, Germany, Belgium
2.	Allowed to revalue, but taxation would result; consequently this prevents revaluation	France
3.	Frequent tax-exempt revaluations	Greece (sometimes Spain, Italy)
4.	Allowed to revalue and no recognition of deferred tax (e.g. because of roll-over relief)	UK
5.	Allowed to revalue, which is followed by accounting for deferred tax	Netherlands

---

EXTRACT 20. SHAREHOLDERS' EQUITY AND LIABILITIES IN THE CONSOLIDATED BALANCE SHEET OF THE AEG GROUP, 1988 (DM MILLION)

Equity:		
Subscribed capital	931	
Capital reserves	885	
Revenue reserves	86	
Net profit of AEG AG	9	
Minority interests	78	
		1,989
Special Untaxed Reserves		5
Accruals		
Accruals for pensions and similar obligations	2,679	
Other accruals	1,851	
		4,530
Financial Liabilities		598
Other Liabilities		
Trade payables	1,068	
Payables to affiliated companies	582	
Other liabilities	604	
		2,254
		9,376

Shown above is the capital and liabilities side of a German consolidated balance sheet. The very large figure for 'other accruals' (*sonstige Rückstellungen*) cannot be for accruals in the UK sense, for this would be some minor year-end adjustments such as unpaid wages or electricity bills. Such amounts would be shown as a last item in a German balance sheet (*Rechnungsabgrenzungsposten*). The expression 'other accruals' is a further example of inevitable pitfalls in translation.

The question here is to what extent are the provisions like those 'provisions for contingencies' discussed earlier, i.e. how many are really reserves. The fact that the profit has been smoothed to zero suggests that 'other accruals' is at least partly the recipient of the other half of the double entries designed to achieve this. Unfortunately, it is impossible to disentangle the total; some of it is presumably for 'contingencies' that would also be recognised in the UK.

The 'accruals for pensions' are not part of shareholders' funds. In a UK company, they would be separately held in a pension trust or in an independent company. A complication arises in that the pension fund may in some countries be over- or under-provided. If it is over-provided, part of it is really reserves. This is discussed above. Incidentally, if DM 2+ billion

TABLE 20.   CALCULATION OF SHAREHOLDERS' FUNDS FOR THE AEG GROUP, 1988 (DM MILLION)

Subscribed capital	931
Capital reserves	885
Revenue reserves	86
Net profit of AEG AG	9
Special untaxed reserves	5*
Other accruals	?
	?

* Or after deduction of corporation tax.

of the provisions are for pensioners, this implies that DM 2+ billion of the total assets (and the income on them) are for pensioners.

Starting from the top of the 'equity' in the AEG balance sheet, it is clear that the first four items are part of shareholders' funds (Table 20). The implication of the order of items is that 'minority interests' are also part of shareholders' funds. However, this results from the German 'entity view' that sees the parent shareholders and the minority shareholders as joint contributors to the capital. For analysts from most countries, minorities are excluded.

Next comes 'special untaxed reserves'. These are amounts that have been charged against income in order to obtain a tax relief. They were not commercial expenses, so they are indeed 'reserves' in UK terminology. They should form part of shareholders' funds. There is one question, though: is it relevant that they would be taxable if they were to be returned back through the income statement in order to be distributed as dividends? If so, the tax rate on distributed income should be deducted (36% at the time of writing). As seen in the following extract, the Swedish accountancy body does think it relevant. However, we could also ask: does the fact that a company cannot distribute share capital mean that the latter is not part of shareholders' funds? In other words: what is the relevance here of distributability or distribution?

Adjustments
Swedish financial statements can be basically adjusted to reflect US accounting principles as follows:

Increase reported net income by 48% of the year's transfers to untaxed reserves; and

Increase reported shareholders' equity by 48% of untaxed reserves in the balance sheet.

52% of each of these items represents deferred taxes. (*The Concise Key to Understanding Swedish Financial Statements*, FAR, 1986)

An analyst is obviously in difficulty here, but the calculation shown here summarises the discussion. Looking on the brighter side, since it is impossible to arrive at a useful profit number in this case, it does not matter that we cannot calculate shareholders' funds!

VII. JAPANESE ACCOUNTS: A SPECIAL CASE

So far, this book has concentrated on the UK, US and continental Europe. However, there is now growing awareness that Japan is an increasingly dominant industrial and financial power, and that we will also need to come to terms with its accounting.[1]

Understanding Japan

As usual, the way to start for the best understanding is to study a little history and the international context. Japanese accounting in the 1990s is a product of a native medieval double-entry bookkeeping system, a borrowing from German and French commercial legal codes in the late nineteenth century, and US-inspired securities legislation of the post-war period.

This tells us to expect some unique features in Japanese statutory accounts, some traditional German-style features and some US-style features. Some examples are as follows:

German-style features

- Control of accounting by government ministries.
- Lack of public availability of accounts of private companies.
- Uniform formats for published accounts, complete with Roman numerals etc., similar to the 1965 German Aktiengesetz which formed the basis of the Fourth Directive.
- Dominance of tax rules in the determination of depreciation and various other provisions. In practice, 'accounting' for deferred tax is not important and is rarely found. Special accelerated depreciation for tax purposes is also recorded in the accounts.
- Strict historical cost for the valuation of fixed assets (also a US feature).
- Dominance of form over substance, and lack of overriding 'fairness' principle, e.g. no capitalisation of leases.
- Proposed dividends not accrued at year ends (also a US feature). Directors' bonuses also not accrued.
- The requirement to create a legal reserve amounting to 25% of share capital (10% in Germany).

[1] I am grateful, for help with this chapter, to Professor S. Maeda of Masashi University, Tokyo, who co-authored an article on which this chapter is based.

- Lack of full provision for pensions; Japanese companies accrue between 40% and 100% of severance indemnities, usually following the tax rules.
- Use of a version of the temporal method for currency translation of foreign financial statements.

US-style features

- Special rules for publicly traded companies (following Securities and Exchange Laws).
- Full consolidated accounts for publicly traded companies; use of equity method for associates and unconsolidated subsidiaries (only recent practice for Germany).
- US order of items in financial statements, e.g. current assets first in balance sheet, and 'cost of sales' format for profit and loss account.
- Consolidated funds flow statements for some publicly traded companies, as recommended by the Japanese Institute of Certified Public Accountants (JICPA).
- Amortisation of goodwill (an option in Germany).
- Use of US (not UK) terminology in translated annual reports.
- Disclosure of earnings per share.

Other features

Except in the few cases noted, the German-style features of Japanese accounting are not found in the US or in the UK; and the US-style features are not found in Germany. Some Japanese practices which fit with neither Germany nor the US are:

- Ability to capitalise research and development expenditure.
- Use of historical exchange rates for translation of non-current foreign currency monetary assets and liabilities in the balance sheets of individual companies.
- Items in the financial statement tend also to be shown as percentages of total assets (balance sheet) or sales (income statement). Some European companies do this.

Regulatory context

There is a Commercial Code in Japan based on an old German model. It is under the control of the Ministry of Justice. All companies must follow this. Public companies (KK, *kabushiki kaisha*; joint stock company) are required to follow stricter rules within the Code. There are about one million KK companies. The Code was traditionally oriented towards the protection of creditors, but shareholders are now considered also. Independent audit is only required by the Commercial Code for large companies. Consolidated accounts are not required, nor are corresponding figures for the previous year.

The second government source of influence is tax law, which has special rules, partly to carry out industrial policies. These rules differ in some important respects from what might be regarded as 'fair' accounting, as discussed in several places in this chapter.

A third form of government influence is through the Securities and Exchange Law modelled on US precedents. This applies to publicly traded companies (about 2,400). This Law requires independent audit and extensive public filing of documents, including consoldiated accounts. Directly related to this is government influence through the Business Accounting Deliberation Council (BADC) which is a committee that advises the Ministry of Finance. This body is perhaps closest by analogy to the French Conseil National de la Comptabilité, in that it has mostly non-government members from many relevant backgrounds. The BADC issues principles which are binding on companies whose securities are publicly traded.

Since the Commercial Code has different requirements from the above more recent source of rules, publicly traded companies must prepare (1) individual company accounts under the Commercial Code, as well as (2) individual and group accounts under the Securities Law using BADC principles. Largely, the differences in rules in the two sources have been removed for parent company accounts.

Moreover, international influences are still strong, so some companies produce yet further versions of their accounts with some or all of the following adjustments:

- In English (or, more likely, 'American' English)
- In dollars as well as yen
- Adjusted for US GAAP or IAS standards.

In particular, Japanese companies that are registered with the SEC in the USA must produce English-language financial statements which must either follow US GAAP or be reconciled to it. Other Japanese companies may also prepare 'convenience translations' for foreigners. However, although these translated accounts approximately follow Japanese rules, they are non-statutory accounts. So, they may show greater or less disclosure than would be required for statutory accounts, and items may be reclassified. Consequently, although these translated accounts may be the only accessible information for those who cannot read Japanese, they do not always provide an accurate representation of proper Japanese accounting. We will now demonstrate this, using the example of Fujitsu KK.

Fujitsu is a public company which is listed on the Tokyo Stock Exchange. It is a telecommunications, computer and microelectronics company with subsidiaries all over the world. Its turnover in 1989 was over $18 billion. We examine here the annual report that is available to the English-speaking public.

Fujitsu: an example of Japanese accounting

The annual report has the following main contents:

1. President's statement
2. Report of operations
3. List of directors
4. List of subsidiaries
5. Consolidated balance sheet (two years)
6. Consolidated income statement (five years)
7. Consolidated funds flow statement (five years)
8. Notes on the above
9. Auditors' report
10. Parent company accounts, as for points 5 to 9.

The funds flow statements are voluntary, and prepared in accordance with the recommendations of the accountancy body (JICPA). The accounts are not those based on the Commercial Code, nor are they exactly as delivered to the Ministry of Finance, but certain items are 'reclassified for the convenience of readers outside Japan' (p. 34). This is here designated a convenience translation (CT).

The original statutory accounts (SA) for 1988 (which illustrate more points than those of 1989 do, e.g. extraordinary items) have been obtained and translated into English. The contents of the statutory reports are different from those of the annual report listed above. Overall there is **less** detail in SA than in CT. This is because group accounts have traditionally been seen as less important in Japan. SA contains:

1. List of main subsidiaries
2. Summary of consolidated operations
3. Consolidated balance sheet (two years)
4. Consolidated income statement (two years)
5. Consolidated statement of appropriation of earnings (two years)
6. Accounting policies
7. Auditors' report.

The total assets, total liabilities and total income are the same in SA as in CT; as the company says, there is merely format reclassification. This can be seen in the CT and translated SA income statements shown in Extracts 21 and 22. A comparison of the statements shows that, although sales, cost of sales and net income are the same, many other figures are different. For example:

EXTRACT 21.   CT: CONSOLIDATED INCOME STATEMENT OF FUJITSU FOR YEAR TO 31 MARCH 1988 (YEN MILLION): EXTRACT FROM FUJITSU 'CONVENIENCE TRANSLATION'

Net sales	2,046,802
Operating costs and expenses:	
Cost of goods sold	1,339,183
Selling, general and administrative expenses	588,098
	1,927,281
Operating income	119,521
Other (income)/expenses:	
Interest charges	28,680
Interest received	(8,923)
Dividends received	(1,557)
Other, net	(4,727)
	13,473
Income before income taxes	106,048
Income taxes	73,407
Equity in income of unconsolidated subsidiaries and affiliates	12,860
	45,501
Minority interests in income of consolidated subsidiaries	3,386
Net income	42,115

1. Gross profit is not shown in CT.
2. Operating income in CT is 13% larger than in SA. This is because 'selling, general and administrative expenses' in SA include the related amounts of business enterprise tax (a tax which is normally about 20% of total corporate income tax). This is not explained in the notes.
3. Other net income and exchange losses come to a **debit** of yen 3,742 million in SA but other net income is a **credit** of yen 4,727 million in CT (because of the treatment of extraordinary items; see point 4).
4. Extraordinary items and taxes on them, including the related business enterprise tax, are shown in SA but not in CT, presumably because they would not be extraordinary under US GAAP.
5. As a result of points 2 and 4, income before taxes is different.
6. 'Corporate income tax and inhabitant tax' in SA amount to **less** than

EXTRACT 22. SA: TRANSLATION OF THE SECURITIES LAW CONSOLIDATED INCOME STATE-MENT OF FUJITSU FOR YEAR TO 31 MARCH 1988 (YEN MILLION)

I.	Sales		2,046,802	100.0
II.	Cost of goods sold		1,339,183	65.4
	Gross profit from sales		707,619	34.6
III.	Selling, general and administrative expenses		601,954	29.4
	Operating profit		105,665	5.2
IV.	Non-operating income			
	1. Interest income and			
	dividend income	10,480		
	2. Other income	15,547	26,027	1.3
V.	Non-operating expenses			
	1. Interest expenses and discount charges	28,680		
	2. Foreign exchange losses	3,982		
	3. Other expenses	15,307	47,969	2.4
	Ordinary income		83,723	4.1
VI.	Extraordinary gains			
	Gain on sale of subsidiaries' shares		8,469	0.4
VII.	Extraordinary losses			
	Business enterprise tax on gain on sale of			
	subsidiaries' shares		1,200	0.1
	Income before taxes		90,992	4.4
	Corporate income tax and inhabitant tax		58,351	2.8
	Minority interests in income of			
	consolidated subsidiaries		3,386	0.1
	Equity in income of unconsolidated			
	subsidiaries and affiliates		12,860	0.6
	Net income		42,115	2.1

'income taxes' in CT. The difference is due to the business enterprise tax (see points 2 and 4) which is included in CT's tax line.
7. Some items are shown in more detail in either SA or CT.

In the balance sheets (not shown here), the difference between CT and SA is mainly a matter of disaggregation. Sometimes CT is more detailed, sometimes SA. For example, CT shows four subheadings under tangible fixed assets (gross), with one total of accumulated depreciation. SA shows five headings (all net); the depreciation amounts are shown in the notes.

EXTRACT 23.   ILLUSTRATIONS OF ACCOUNTING POLICIES (BY NOTE NUMBER) IN FUJITSU'S 1989 REPORT

1(a)   *Basis of presenting consolidated financial statements*
The accompanying consolidated financial statements have been prepared in accordance with accounting principles and practices generally accepted in Japan, and from the consolidated financial statements filed with the Ministry of Finance in Japan (MOF). Certain items presented in the consolidated financial statements filed with MOF have been reclassified for the convenience of readers outside. Japan. The statements of changes in financial position for the five years ended 31 March 1989 have been prepared for the purpose of inclusion in this annual report in accordance with the method recommended by the Japanese Institute of Certified Public Accountants, although such statements are not customarily prepared in Japan and are not required to be filed with MOF.

Where significant differences exist between the accounting practices which the Fujitsu Group has followed and International Accounting Standards (IAS) which affect net income, these are set out in the relevant notes on accounting policies below.

1(b)   *Principles of consolidation*
The excess of the purchase price over the value of the net assets of businesses acquired is amortised over a reasonable period on the straight-line basis.

1(d)   *Allowance for doubtful accounts*
The allowance for doubtful accounts is provided at an estimated amount of probable bad debts plus the maximum amount which could be charged to income under Japanese income tax law, whereas the accrual assumption in IAS 1 requires provision only for estimated probable bad debts.

1(e)   *Inventories*
Raw materials and purchased components are stated at cost determined by the moving average method and the most recent purchase price method, respectively . . . IAS 2 requires that inventories be valued at the lower of historical cost and net realisable value. The aggregate value of inventories would not have been significantly different if IAS 2 had been applied.

1(f)   *Property, plant and equipment, and depreciation*
Property, plant and equipment, including significant renewals and additions, are carried at cost.

1(g)   *Accrued severance indemnities and pension plan*
Employees who terminated their service with the Fujitsu Group are generally entitled to lump-sum severance indemnities determined by reference to current basic rates of pay and length of service. Severance indemnities are not funded. The Fujitsu Group has in general provided for this liability to the extent of 50% of the amount which would be required if all employees voluntarily terminated their service at the balance sheet date, whereas the accrual assumption in IAS 1 requires the accrual of 100% of the above-mentioned amount.

1(k)   *Income taxes*
Income taxes have been accrued on the basis of actual income tax liabilities and

no provision is made for deferred taxes arising from timing differences between financial and tax reporting, whereas IAS 12 requires inter-period tax allocation.

1(l)   *Translation of foreign currency accounts*
Current receivables and payables denominated in foreign currencies are translated into Japanese yen at exchange rates in effect at the respective balance sheet dates. Non-current receivables and payables denominated in foreign currencies are translated into Japanese yen at historical exchange rates.

The accounts of foreign subsidiaries, minor in consolidation, are translated into Japanese yen at applicable year-end rates. Income and expenses are translated at the average rate during the year.

1(n)   *Legal reserve*
The Japanese Commercial Code provides that an amount not less than 10% of cash dividends paid be appropriated as a legal reserve until such reserve equals 25% of stated capital. The legal reserve may be used to reduce a deficit or may be transferred to stated capital, but is not available for distribution as dividends.

8   *Intangible assets*
Intangible assets are mainly amortised over five years on the straight-line basis.

11   *Research and development expenses*
Research and development expenses are included in selling, general and administrative expenses.

Most of the totals (e.g. current assets, retained earnings) are the same in both balance sheets, although the current versus non-current liabilities are very slightly differently divided.

Accounting policies

Given that the income and net assets figures are the same for CT as for SA, the accounting policies must be very similar in CT to those for statutory Japanese accounting. Some of these features were listed in the first section. These are illustrated in Extract 23 by quotations from Fujitsu's 1989 Report. Some of Fujitsu's policies need comment:

Currency translation   A version of the temporal method is normally required, but because Fujitsu's amounts are 'minor' it can use the closing rate method.
Pensions   Fujitsu provides for only 50% of severance indemnities.
R & D   This could be capitalised under certain circumstances.

As one would expect, Japanese accounting is different from that of any other country. However, again as with any other country, there are many international influences, those of Germany and the USA being the most obvious. Those interested in Japanese annual reports will find that: **Conclusions**

1. For most companies (except publicly traded companies) none is publicly available.
2. For untraded KK companies, accounts drawn up under the Commercial Code are available to stockholders and creditors (unconsolidated, lacking in detail, tax influenced).
3. For publicly traded companies there are Securities Law/BADC accounts publicly available.
4. For internationally oriented companies there may also be translated accounts, and possibly accounts adjusted towards IASC or US GAAP rules.
5. For SEC-registered companies, there will be reconciliations with US GAAP.

In the case of Fujitsu, we have been examining SA (type 3) and CT (type 4). This reveals that SA is different in classification from CT, which significantly affects income statement interpretation. Also CT, and therefore SA even more so, is different from UK or other national practices. The principal differences from normal UK practice for large companies are:

- Property is carried at cost.
- Goodwill is capitalised and amortised.
- Bad debt provisions are set at the maximum allowed by tax rules.
- Stock is usually valued at cost rather than at net realisable value if lower.
- Pensions are not fully accrued for.
- Depreciation is based on the same rules as tax rules.
- Non-current debtors and creditors in foreign currencies are translated at historical rates.
- A legal reserve is established.
- Proposed dividends are not accrued.
- US-style formats are used for balance sheets.
- US terminology prevails.
- A version of the temporal method is used for foreign subsidiaries' accounts.

VIII. HARMONISATION: WORLD AND EUROPE

The preceding chapters make it clear that there are major differences in the financial reporting practices of companies in different countries, particularly between Anglo-Saxon countries and continental Europe. This leads to great complications for those preparing, consolidating, auditing and interpreting published financial statements. To combat this, several organisations throughout the world are involved in attempts to harmonise or standardise accounting.

This chapter starts by looking at the purposes of and obstacles to standardisation. There follow sections on the work of the IASC and other international bodies. Finally, there is a section on the nature and progress of harmonisation in the EC and a summary.

Reasons for harmonisation

It is increasingly the case that the products of accounting in one country are used in various other countries. Consequently, the reasons that make national accounting standards desirable also apply internationally. The pressure for international harmonisation comes from those who regulate, prepare and use financial statements. We will now look at their interests more closely.

Investors and financial analysts
Investors and financial analysts need to be able to understand the financial statements of foreign companies whose shares they might wish to buy. They would like to be sure that statements from different countries are reliable and comparable, or at least to be clear about the nature and magnitude of the differences. They also need confidence in the soundness of the auditing.

UN and EC
For this reason, various intergovernmental transnational bodies from the EC Commission to the United Nations are interested, among other things, in protecting investors within their spheres of influence. Also, in cases where foreign shares are quoted on the domestic stock exchange of an investor, that stock exchange will often demand financial statements which are consistent with domestic practices. In addition, those companies which wish to issue new shares more widely than on their domestic

Reasons for and obstacles to harmonisation

markets will see the advantages of standardised practices in the pro-
motion of their issues.

Multinationals

These pressures will also be felt by companies which do not operate
multinationally. However, for multinationals the advantages of harmonisation are much more important. The great effort of financial accountants
to prepare and consolidate financial statements would be much simplified
if statements from all round the world were prepared on the same basis.
Similarly, the task of preparing comparable internal information for the
appraisal of the performance of subsidiaries in different countries would
be made much easier. Many aspects of investment appraisal, performance evaluation, and other decision-making uses of management
accounting information would benefit from harmonisation. The appraisal
of foreign companies for potential takeovers would also be greatly facili-
tated. Multinational companies would also find it easier to transfer
accounting staff from one country to another.

Accountancy firms

A third group which would benefit from harmonisation is the international
accountancy firms. Many of the clients of the large Anglo-American
accountancy firms have at least one foreign subsidiary or branch. The
preparation, consolidation and auditing of these companies' financial
statements would become less onerous if accounting practices were
harmonised. Also, the accountancy firms would benefit from the added
mobility of staff.

Tax authorities

The revenue authorities throughout the world have their work greatly
complicated, when dealing with foreign incomes, by differences in the
measurement of profit in different countries. It should be admitted,
however, that revenue authorities have **caused** many of the differences,
for example the influence of tax on continental accounting (see Chapter III)
and the use of LIFO in the United States (see Chapter II).

Other groups

Governments in developing countries might find it easier to understand
and control the operations of multinationals if financial reporting were
harmonised, particularly as this would imply greater disclosure in some
cases. International credit grantors like the World Bank must also face the
difficulties of comparison. Other organisations that would benefit from
greater international comparability of company information are the labour
unions that face multinational employers. All these groups might benefit
from harmonisation.

Obstacles to harmonisation

The most fundamental of obstacles to harmonisation is the size of the present differences between the accounting practices of different countries. Using the type of classifications of accounting systems discussed in Chapter III, there are several significant differences even within the Anglo-Saxon class, let alone between that class and the Franco-German. These latter differences go to the root of the reasons for the preparation of accounting information. The general dichotomy between shareholder/fair-view presentation and creditor/tax/conservative presentation is an obstacle sufficiently difficult not to be overcome without major changes in attitudes and law.

Indeed, it is not clear that it **should be** overcome. If the predominant purposes of financial reporting vary by country, it seems reasonable that the reporting should vary. However, harmonisation is concerned with similar users who receive information from companies in different countries. It may be that the relevant companies should be required to produce two sets of financial statements: one for domestic and another for international consumption. This is discussed further later in this chapter.

Another obstacle is the lack of strong professional accountancy bodies in some countries. This means that any body such as the IASC, which seeks to operate through national accountancy bodies, will not be effective in all countries. The alternative to this, a worldwide enforcement agency, is also lacking. The EC Commission may prove to be such an agency for one part of the world, as is discussed later.

A further problem is nationalism. This may show itself in an unwillingness to accept compromises which involve changing accounting practices towards those of other countries. This unwillingness may exist on the part of accountants and companies or on the part of states who may not wish to lose their sovereignty. Another manifestation of nationalism may be the lack of knowledge of or interest in accounting elsewhere. A rather more subtle and acceptable variety of this is the concern that it would be difficult to alter internationally set standards in response to a change of mind or a change of circumstances.

These are the major general obstacles to international harmonisation. The following sections look at the progress of several organisations in

TABLE 21. CLASSIFICATION OF SOME ACCOUNTING HARMONISERS		
	World	*Regional*
Government	UN, OECD	EC
Professional	IASC	FEE

overcoming them. Many harmonising agencies have already been discussed in this chapter, and discussion of a few more will follow. Before launching into further detail, it will be useful to classify agencies by authority and by geographical scope, as in Table 21. This table is not exhaustive; as we shall see, there are other regional bodies.

The International Accounting Standards Committee

History and purpose of the IASC

Of the many bodies working for international standardisation to be looked at in this chapter, the IASC is perhaps the most important and the most successful (apart from the EC Commission, which operates in a more restricted area). The IASC was founded in 1973 and has a small secretariat based in London. The original board members were the accountancy bodies of nine countries: Australia, Canada, France, Japan, Mexico, The Netherlands, the United Kingdom, Ireland, the United States and West Germany. Most of these, plus the bodies of several other countries, make up the main board of the IASC (Table 22). In 1990 there were about 100 member accountancy bodies from about 80 countries.

The aim of the IASC is 'to formulate and publish in the public interest accounting standards to be observed in the presentation of financial statements and to promote their worldwide acceptance and observance' (IASC *Objectives and Procedures*, 1982; the word 'basic' preceded the words 'accounting standards' in the original 1973 version). The member bodies of IASC agree to support the standards and to use 'their best endeavours' to ensure that published financial statements comply with the standards; to ensure that auditors enforce this; and to persuade governments, stock exchanges and other bodies to back the standards.

The Standards

A list of IASC standards is shown in Table 23. These are preceded by

TABLE 22.	BOARD MEMBERS OF IASC, 1990
Australia	Netherlands
Canada	South Africa
Denmark	United Kingdom
France	United States
Germany	International Coordinating
Italy	Committee of Financial Analysts
Japan	Associations
Jordan	
Korea	

exposure drafts prepared by subcommittees of the board. In order to be published, an exposure draft must be approved by a two-thirds majority of the board. A subsequent standard must be approved by a three-quarters majority.

It is the countries influenced by the Anglo-American tradition which are most familiar with setting accounting standards and are most likely to be able to adopt them professionally. It is not surprising, then, that the working language of the IASC is English, that its secretariat is in London, that nearly all the chairmen and secretaries-general have been from countries using Anglo-American or Dutch accounting, and that most standards either closely follow or compromise between US and UK standards.

Consequently, the IASC's standards generally allow a range of practices. For example, research and development expenditure may be carried forward according to IAS 9 under similar conditions to those in SSAP 13, whereas such expenditure cannot be carried forward under SFAS 2. Similarly, IAS 12 allows partial allocation for deferred tax, like SSAP 15, whereas APB Opinion 11 requires comprehensive allocation.

However, there are some cases where international standards are more demanding with regard to disclosure. For example, IAS 9 calls for disclosure of the year's R&D expenses (paragraph 23), whereas the original SSAP 13 did not. However, the US standard calls for greater disclosure than the UK standard did, which helps to explain why the international standard also does.

The original intention of the IASC was to avoid complex detail and to concentrate on basic standards. However, the list of standards includes some, like 'Accounting for construction contracts' (IAS 11), which might not be thought to be 'basic'. Further, the contents of some standards could be criticised as being unnecessarily detailed. For example, the details for the ascertainment of net realisable value (paragraphs 28–31 of IAS 2) could be thought excessive in the context of the great diversity of practice on much more fundamental matters within inventory valuation. However, in the author's opinion these are exceptions, and the standards are generally commendably clearly presented.

Important moves to reduce the options in IASC standards were begun in 1989 and will be discussed below.

Enforcement

The success of member accountancy bodies' 'best endeavours' to promote the work of the IASC varies to some degree. The problem is one of enforcement. The IASC has no authority of its own and therefore must rely on that of its members. It has been seen in earlier chapters that the influence of professional accountancy bodies in the formulation of accounting rules also varies widely between countries.

TABLE 23.   IASC STANDARDS (TO EARLY 1990)

Preface (revised January 1983)
Objectives and Procedures (including the constitution; revised October 1982)

IAS   1 Disclosure of accounting policies
IAS   2 Valuation and presentation of inventories in the context of the historical cost system
IAS   3 Consolidated financial statements (superseded by IAS 27)
IAS   4 Depreciation accounting
IAS   5 Information to be disclosed in financial statements
IAS   6 Accounting responses to changing prices (superseded by IAS 15)
IAS   7 Statement of changes in financial position
IAS   8 Unusual and prior period items and changes in accounting policies
IAS   9 Accounting for research and development activities
IAS 10 Contingencies and events occurring after the balance sheet date
IAS 11 Accounting for construction contracts
IAS 12 Accounting for taxes on income
IAS 13 Presentation of current assets and current liabilities
IAS 14 Reporting financial information by segment
IAS 15 Information reflecting the effects of changing prices
IAS 16 Accounting for property, plant and equipment
IAS 17 Accounting for leases
IAS 18 Revenue recognition
IAS 19 Accounting for retirement benefits in the financial statements of employers
IAS 20 Accounting for government grants and disclosure of government assistance
IAS 21 Accounting for the effects of changes in foreign exchange rates
IAS 22 Accounting for business combinations
IAS 23 Capitalisation of borrowing costs
IAS 24 Related party disclosures
IAS 25 Accounting for investments
IAS 26 Accounting and reporting by retirement benefit plans
IAS 27 Consolidated financial statements and accounting for investments in subsidiaries
IAS 28 Accounting for investments in associates
IAS 29 Financial reporting in hyperinflationary economies
IAS 30 Disclosure in the financial statements of banks

France and Germany

In France and Germany, for example, the Ordre and the Institut have little room (and inadequate authority) to influence accounting practice because of the strength and detail of company law and the *plan comptable.* The more powerful bodies like the Conseil National de la Comptabilité or the Commission des Opérations de Bourse are not members of the IASC.

UK

At the other extreme, in the UK, Ireland, New Zealand and Canada, accounting standards were, until 1990 (see Chapter II), set by the professional bodies which belong to the IASC. Consequently it has been possible for the IASC's standards to be introduced. Taking the UK and Ireland as an example, standards are brought into line with IASC standards wherever possible. Standards either state that compliance automatically ensures compliance with the IASC standard, or outline the differences.

USA

In between these two extremes is the United States. The two bodies most directly concerned with the setting and enforcement of domestic standards, the FASB and the SEC, are not members of the IASC. However the AICPA, which is the US representative on the IASC, is influential. Also, the FASB is sympathetic to the work of the IASC, though it does not directly take the IASC's views into account. The FASB and the EC Commission have recently joined the IASC's Consultative Group.

One tell-tale sign of the problems of enforcement is the gradual weakening of the commitments required from member bodies. At one stage, members were required to use their best endeavours to ensure that companies who broke international standards would disclose this fact. Now the IASC *Preface* calls for companies that **observe** the standards to disclose this fact. In the case of the UK and Ireland, the professional bodies have moved away from the idea of audit qualifications for breaches of IASC standards or even for lack of disclosure of breaches. It is probably the case that most UK accountants are not very conversant with the content or status of IASC standards.

Italy

There is probably some IASC influence in other continental European countries. The most obvious example is in Italy, where listed companies (a small but important group) are required to follow IASC standards. This is part of a major change towards Anglo-Saxon types of financial reporting and auditing for listed and state companies in Italy.

Further IASC benefits

There has also been IASC influence in the move towards consolidated accounting in continental Europe (see Chapter V). Anglo-Dutch consolidation practices are clearly predominant in the EC's Seventh Directive on company law, which requires consolidation. However, it was useful to be able to point to the internationally agreed IAS 3 on the subject; and countries such as France have enthusiastically moved towards adoption of consolidation on that basis, whereas they might have found it more difficult if this were seen as 'following the UK'.

More generally, there may be great long-term benefit from bringing together senior accountants from major countries to discuss technical and theoretical problems. The enhanced level of understanding of each other's practices should assist harmonisation eventually, perhaps via a different agency such as the EC Commission.

Developing countries

There is a second major area where we may look for IASC achievements towards the underlying aim of harmonisation. For those developing countries that did not have accounting standards, a ready-made IASC set has proved attractive. It can be adapted to local conditions as necessary. Kenya, Malaysia, Nigeria, Pakistan, Singapore and Zimbabwe fit into this category. It is obviously preferable for them to adopt (in whole or part) an internationally recognised set of standards, from a body to which they belong, rather than to follow the standards of any one country. However, the six countries named have a feature in common: they have inherited a British legal and commercial structure. This makes it less surprising that IASC standards seem suitable to them; perhaps they would have followed similar UK standards anyway, though that path might have been slower and less comfortable for them. An important point in this context is whether IASC standards are suitable for such countries.

The IASC in the 1990s

In the late 1980s, the IASC began a project (published as E 32) to reduce options within its standards. This was part of a major campaign to increase the IASC's influence. The SEC and IOSCO (International Organisation of Securities Commissions) had given the IASC some encouragement that they might support its standards for use by foreign registrants on national stock exchanges, but only if IASC standards became more precise. Since the options in IASs had been included in order to enable international agreement, the process of removing them has been painful. Furthermore, many observers doubted whether the SEC would ever give up its own regulations, especially for the much less detailed IASs. Nevertheless, it is clear that the IASC is becoming increasingly important in the eyes of stock exchanges, the IOSCO and the EC Commission.

This section looks at the nature and importance of some other bodies concerned with international aspects of accounting.

International Federation of Accountants (IFAC)

This body came into being in 1977 after the Eleventh International Congress of Accountants. It aims to develop a coordinated international accountancy profession. A predecessor body, called the International Coordination Committee for the Accountancy Profession, which had been formed in 1972 after the Tenth Congress, was wound up in favour of the IFAC.

The IFAC has a full-time secretariat in New York and comprises an assembly of the same accountancy bodies as belong to the IASC. Its work includes the setting of international guidelines for auditing (via the International Auditing Practices Committee), ethics, education and management accounting; involvement in education and technical research; and organising the international congress about every five years.

Fédération des Experts Comptables Européens (FEE)

The FEE started work at the beginning of 1987, taking over from two earlier European bodies: the Groupe d'Etudes (formed in 1966) and the Union Européenne des Experts Comptables.

FEE is based in Brussels and has member accountancy bodies throughout Europe. Its interests include auditing, accounting and taxation. It studies international differences and tries to contribute to their removal. Much of its work is connected with the EC, and it advises the EC Commission on company law and accounting harmonisation. If FEE can arrive at a consensus of European accountants this gives it a powerful voice in Brussels, particularly if governments are disagreeing. One of FEE's predecessors (the Groupe d'Etudes) seems to have accepted the dominance of 'true and fair' and the need for consolidation; this may have helped in their acceptance by the Commission.

Non-accounting bodies

One of the factors that drives accountants and their professional bodies towards better national and international standards is the possibility that other bodies will intervene or gain the initiative. At present, with the regional exception of the EC Commission, such international bodies have influence rather than power. The Organisation for Economic Cooperation and Development (OECD) has researched and adopted recommendations for accounting practice: the *Guidelines for Multinational Enterprises.* These mainly concern disclosure requirements. They are voluntary, but they may influence the behaviour of large and politically sensitive corporations. Since 1976 there has been a survey of accounting practices, but no agreement as to how to achieve harmonisation.

It seems clear that part of the OECD's aim in this area is to protect developed countries from any extreme proposals that might come from the United Nations, which is interested in the regulation of multinational businesses. In 1977 the UN published a report in this area which proposed very substantial increases in disclosure of financial and non-financial items by transnational corporations. The UN went further and set up an Intergovernmental Group on International Accounting Standards and Reporting, which intended to publish standards for multinational companies. However, progress has been slow, perhaps partly because of differences of stance towards multinationals between host and parent countries.

EC harmonisation

Reasons for and obstacles to EC harmonisation

The objects of the Treaty of Rome (of 1957) include the establishment of the free movement of persons, goods and services, and capital. This involves the elimination of customs duties, the imposition of common tariffs to third countries and the establishment of procedures to permit the coordination of economic policies. More specifically, the EC's Common Industrial Policy (of 1970) calls for the creation of a unified business environment, including the harmonisation of company law and taxation, and the creation of a common capital market.

The reasoning behind these objectives includes the fact that the activities of companies extend beyond national frontiers, and that shareholders and others need protection throughout the EC. In order to achieve this and to encourage the movement of capital, it is necessary to create a flow of reliable financial information about companies from all parts of the EC. Further, since companies in different EC countries exist in the same form and are in competition with each other, it is argued that they should be subject to the same laws and taxation.

The obstacles to harmonisation of financial reporting and company law have been discussed earlier in this chapter. Of particular importance here are the fundamental differences between the various national accounting systems in the EC. They include the differences between creditor/secrecy in the Franco-German systems and investor/disclosure in the Anglo-Dutch systems, and between law-based/tax-based rules and professionally set standards. These large differences have contributed towards the great variations in the size and strength of the profession. The smaller and weaker professional bodies in Franco-German countries are an obstacle to movements towards accounting and auditing of an Anglo-Dutch type (see Chapter III).

Directives and regulations

The EC Commission achieves its harmonising objectives through two main instruments: Directives, which must be incorporated into the laws of member states; and Regulations, which become law throughout the EC without the need to pass through national legislatures. The concern of this section will be with the Directives on company law and with two Regulations. These are listed in Table 24 with a brief description of their scope. The company law Directives of most relevance to accounting are the Fourth and Seventh (see, also, Chapter V for the latter). The Fourth will be discussed in more detail below, after an outline of the procedure for setting Directives.

First, the Commission, which is the EC's permanent civil service, decides on a project and asks an expert to prepare a report. In the case of the Fourth Directive, this was the Elmendorff Report of 1967. Then an *avant projet* or discussion document is prepared. This is studied by a Commission working party and commented on by FEE. This may lead to the issuing of a draft Directive, which is commented on by the European Parliament (a directly elected assembly with limited powers) and the Economic and Social Committee (a consultative body of employers, employees and others). A revised proposal is then submitted to a working party of the Council of Ministers. The Council, consisting of the relevant ministers from each EC country, must vote unanimously if a Directive or Regulation is to be adopted. In the case of a Directive, member states are required to introduce a national law within a specified period, though they often exceed it, as discussed below in the case of the Fourth Directive.

The Fourth Directive
The exact effects of any Directive on a particular country will depend upon the laws passed by national legislatures. For example, there are dozens of provisions in the Fourth Directive which begin with such expressions as 'member states may require or permit companies to . . .'. Given this flexibility, the effects on the accounting of different countries have been included in the relevant chapters. However, it seems appropriate to consider here the general outline of the Directive and the process whereby it took its ultimate form.

The Directive covers public and private companies in all EC countries. Its articles include those referring to valuation rules, formats of published financial statements and disclosure requirements. It does not cover consolidation, which is left for the Seventh Directive. The Fourth Directive's first draft was published in 1971, before the UK, Ireland and Denmark had entered the EC or had representatives on the Groupe d'Etudes. This initial draft was heavily influenced by German company law, particularly the Aktiengesetz of 1965. Consequently, valuation rules were to be conservative, formats were to be prescribed in rigid detail, and disclosure by notes

TABLE 24.	EC DIRECTIVES AND REGULATIONS RELEVANT TO CORPORATE ACCOUNTING (TO MID-1990)			
	Draft dates	*Date adopted*	*UK law*	*Topic*
Directives on company law				
First	1964	1968	1972	*Ultra vires* rules
Second	1970,1972	1976	1980	Separation of public companies, minimum capital, distributions
Third	1970,1973, 1975	1978	1987	Mergers
Fourth	1971,1974	1978	1981	Formats and rules of accounting
Fifth	1972,1983			Structure, management and audit of companies
Sixth	1978	1982	1987	De-mergers
Seventh	1976,1978	1983	1989	Consolidated accounting
Eighth	1978	1984	1989	Qualifications and work of auditors
Ninth	–			Links between public company groups
Tenth	1985			International mergers of public companies
Eleventh	1986			Disclosures about branches
Twelfth	1988			Single member company
Thirteenth	1989			Takeovers
Vredeling	1980,1983			Employee information and consultation
Regulations				
Societas Europea	1970,1975, 1989			European company subject to EC laws
European economic interest grouping	1973,1978	1985		Business form for multi-national joint ventures

was to be very limited. Financial statements were to obey the provisions of the Directive.

The influence of the UK and Ireland on the EC Commission, Parliament and Groupe d'Etudes was such that a much amended draft was issued in 1974. This introduced the concept of the 'true and fair view'. Another change by 1974 was that some flexibility of presentation had been introduced. This process continued and, by the promulgation of the finalised Directive, the 'true and fair view' was established as a predominant principle in the preparation of financial statements (Article 2, paragraphs 2–5). In addition, the four principles of the UK's SSAP 2 (accruals, prudence, consistency and going concern) were made clearer than they had been in the 1974 draft (Article 31).

More rearrangement and summarisation of items in the financial statements were made possible (Article 4). There were also calls for more notes in the 1974 draft than in the 1971 draft, and more in the final Directive than in the 1974 draft (Articles 43–46). Another concern of Anglo-Dutch accountants has been with the effect of taxation on Franco-German accounts. The extra disclosures called for by the 1974 draft about the effect of taxation are included in the final Directive (Articles 30 and 35).

The fact that member states may permit or require a type of inflation accounting is treated in more detail in the final Directive than in the 1974 draft (Article 33). As a further accommodation of Anglo-Dutch opinion, a Contact Committee of EC and national civil servants is provided for. This was intended to answer the criticism that the Directive will give rise to laws which are not sensitive to changing circumstances and attitudes. The Committee looks at practical problems arising from the implementation of the Directive, and makes suggestions for amendments (Article 52).

The Fourth Directive was supposed to be enacted in member states by July 1980 and to be in force by January 1982. No country managed the former date, as may be seen in Table 25.

The implementation in the UK was brought about by the 1981 Companies Act. The changes included compulsory formats and detailed valua-

TABLE 25. IMPLEMENTATION OF EC ACCOUNTING DIRECTIVES AS LAWS		
	Fourth	*Seventh*
Denmark	1981	1990
UK	1981	1989
France	1983	1985
Netherlands	1983	1988
Luxembourg	1984	1988
Belgium	1985	1990
Germany	1985	1985
Ireland	1986	–
Greece	1986	1987
Spain	1989	1989
Portugal	1989	–
Italy	–	–

tion requirements, which also affect The Netherlands and Ireland in a similar way. In other countries the introduction of the 'true and fair view' as an overriding requirement, the requirements for extra disclosures, and the extension of publication and audit in many more companies were significant.

It is clear that neither asset valuation, nor formats, nor disclosure have been completely standardised as a result of the laws consequent upon the Fourth Directive. However, **harmonisation** has been noticeable and inevitable, although UK statements, for example, have been much less affected than was feared by some UK accountants. The present degree of harmonisation might reasonably be welcomed by shareholders and accountants throughout the EC.

Nevertheless, there is a very loose compromise between the opinions of those countries which are in favour of adjustments for price changes (The Netherlands, at one extreme) and those which are against them (Germany, at the other extreme). There is a requirement that the difference between the adjusted figures and historical cost must be shown. However, there is no requirement that all member states must demand at least some adjustment; there will be no standardisation on current cost or current purchasing power adjustments; and there is no direction about whether adjusted statements should be the main or supplementary ones, or whether merely adjusting notes should be provided.

It is particularly in the key area of measurement that a lack of harmonisation remains obvious. In 1990 the EC Commission began moves to try to speed up harmonisation by establishing a forum of European standard setters.

Other directives
The Second Directive concerns a number of matters connected with share capital and the differences between public and private companies. The draft Fifth Directive and the draft Vredeling Directive concern attempts by the Commission to improve the involvement of employees in companies. There are proposals for informing employees and consulting them on important matters, and for employee involvement in the management of public companies. The Seventh Directive concerns consolidated accounting, and is considered in Chapter V. The Eighth Directive was watered down from its original draft, which might have greatly affected the training patterns and scope of work of accountants, particularly in the UK. However, its main effect now is to decide on who is allowed to audit accounts in certain countries that have small numbers of accountants, such as Germany.

Regulations

One of the draft Regulations shown in Table 23 concerns a totally new type of company which will be registered as an EC company and will be subject to EC laws. It will be called the *Societas Europea* (SE). However, despite continued pressure from the Commission, progress has been very slow, partly because member states may not wish to lose sovereignty over companies operating in their countries, and partly because member states have found it difficult to agree upon a company structure with respect to worker participation on boards of directors.

It was easier to agree upon proposals for a form of joint venture organisation for EC companies. The Regulation on the 'European economic interest grouping' is based on the French business form, the *groupement d'intérêt économique* – as used, for example, by Airbus Industrie. It provides a corporate organisation which can be smaller and of shorter duration than the SE. Members of a grouping are autonomous profit-making entities, whereas the grouping itself provides joint facilities or enables a combination for a specific purpose.

Unresolved problems for 1992

Despite all the harmonising work of the EC Commission and the substantial implementation programmes of most member states, much of the problem of different accounting practices remains. For obvious reasons, it may be instructive to choose the date 1992 as a point of reference. By then, the Fourth and Seventh Directives will be implemented and in force in nearly all member states. The differences remaining will include:

Publication and audit   The prevalence of the requirement to publish accounts and to have external audit will still vary throughout the EC. For example, in the UK audit is universal, whereas it is restricted to the minority of large companies in Germany.

Formats and terminology   The different national degrees of choice allowed for formats, and the resulting differences in predominant formats, may make analysis more difficult. To some extent this may seem a trivial problem, but the formats are not convertible into each other in the case of the two styles of profit and loss account. Terminology may also seem a trivial problem, but only a few large companies produce translations, and even these may be misleading. For untranslated accounts, added difficulties are raised for most analysts.

Fixed asset valuation   Despite the Fourth Directive, the European variations in asset valuation remain great. In the UK and The Netherlands, there is a mixture of historical and current values. In France, Italy and Spain, there are revaluations at intervals. In Germany, there is strict historical cost. This makes it difficult to compare net assets, total assets, shareholders' funds or ratios based on these.

Conservatism   Apart from fixed asset valuation, there are also other general differences in bias which have survived harmonisation. For example, there is greater conservatism in German than in UK accounting.

Taxation and fairness   Dispute between tax-based values and commercial values is central to accounting, and to international comparisons. In much of continental Europe, taxation is a dominant influence on accounting numbers. This is not the case in the UK and The Netherlands, and need not be the case for French group accounts.

Consolidation   Even after the considerable harmonisation achieved by the Seventh Directive, many consolidation practices still vary internationally. For example, goodwill is still calculated and disposed of differently; proportional consolidation is used in some countries but not others; subsidiaries are defined differently.

Currency translation   There are few rules on the translation of subsidiaries' accounts in most countries. Many German groups use a version of the temporal method, which is out of line with most of Europe.

Summary

There are many interested parties who would benefit from international harmonisation. These include shareholders, stock exchanges, multinational companies, accounting firms, trade unions and revenue authorities. The scope for standardisation is great because the international variations in practice are very large. However, the obstacles are important, too. The fundamental causes of differences remain and these are backed up by nationalistic inertia. At present, the lack of an international enforcement agency is crucial.

However, a number of bodies are working for harmonisation of accounting rules and disclosure, notably the IASC which has rapidly published a substantial list of international standards. These are heavily influenced by practices in the UK and the US, and have the most effect in English-speaking countries. Enforcement in other areas of the world is difficult because of underdeveloped accountancy professions or because the rules for financial reporting are made by governments. It may be that the development of dual standards for domestic and foreign reporting would be an easier solution, which would preserve differences in accounting that result from national differences of an economic, social and legal nature. The IASC is reducing options in the 1990s.

There are other bodies concerned with harmonisation on a worldwide or regional basis. However, the most powerful source of change towards harmonisation among leading countries in world accounting is the EC Commission. Harmonisation of accounting is one of the many aims of the Commission as part of its overall objective to remove economic barriers within the EC.

Harmonisation is being achieved through EC Directives and Regulations. It is particularly the Fourth and Seventh Directives on company law which have been affecting accounting in Europe. The Fourth Directive has caused important changes in most EC countries in formats of accounts or disclosure or valuation procedures. The Seventh Directive is harmonising consolidation practices. However, partly because of differing opinions among the member states, there are no detailed requirements concerning valuation rules. This will restrict the degree of harmonisation, and is a topic for the 1990s.

IX. INTERNATIONAL ANALYSIS

The problem

The material in this book has shown that there are deep-seated causes of international accounting differences. These differences are very resistant to change, and they will continue for many years to make international comparisons very difficult.

The worst error for analysts is not to realise that the differences are great. The next error is to suppose that they can be adjusted for by simple multipliers or rules of thumb. This book has shown that the world is more complex than that. For example, although German profit numbers are often smaller than UK accountants would have calculated, the degree of understatement varies, and sometimes German profit numbers may be larger.

The only reliable approach is to become well informed about the international differences, and then to adjust for the major items line-by-line. Of course, help can be found in this endeavour. This book has tried to help with the former task (education), and makes preliminary efforts to address the second task (adjustments) in this chapter.

A benchmark

In order to appraise companies, it is normal to place special emphasis on a few accounting aggregates and ratios. In many ways this is particularly dangerous because the commercial world and the companies in it are more complex than can reasonably be encapsulated in a few simple numbers or ratios. For example, the fixation by some analysts on earnings gives rise to efforts by companies to record gains 'above the line', to record losses 'below the line', and to take some items 'off balance sheet'. All these efforts will not be directly connected to the underlying reality of transactions. Despite the fact that the transactions may be well documented in the notes to the financial statements, an analyst who concentrates on a few standard totals and ratios will be misled. Of course, the scope for confusion increases dramatically in multinationals and in international comparisons.

Nevertheless, standard ratios are widely used, and emphasis here will be placed upon adjustments to earnings and net assets. Other figures are either fairly easy to determine (such as the total of current assets, the number of shares outstanding or the market share price) or may be easily derived from the above two key aggregates (such as cash flow or shareholders' equity).

134

TABLE 26.   UK BENCHMARK FOR ADJUSTMENT OF US COMPANIES

Inventories	Use FIFO not LIFO
Deferred tax	Move to partial accounting; assume that deferred tax is a reserve not a liability
Translation	Extract gains and losses from income statement if due to use of temporal method; retain use of average rate for income statement items under current rate method
Fixed assets	Leave at historical cost
Goodwill	Remove any assets and amortisation charges
Excluded subsidiaries	Standardise on inclusion of all subsidiaries, which raises assets and liabilities
Poolings	Standardise on purchase accounting, which would give lower reserves and earnings but higher assets than poolings
Dividends	Note that US companies do not provide for undeclared dividends
Extraordinaries	Treat US gains and losses on the sale of businesses and on major restructuring as extraordinary
Interest capitalisation	Remove any asset and treat as expense
Oil and gas	Standardise on the successful efforts method
R & D	Leave US practices at uniform expensing

It is probable that most readers of this book will find a UK or US benchmark the most useful, not least because the numbers of listed companies are far greater in each of these two countries than in any continental European country. This chapter concentrates on a benchmark which is a version of UK practice. If a US benchmark is preferred, it will merely be necessary to be mindful of Anglo-American differences, as explained in Chapter II.

If we were merely comparing US with UK companies, the choice of benchmark would be easier. Indeed, elements from both countries could be chosen. In some cases, UK practice is so varied or adjustment to a UK practice would be so difficult that it is necessary to settle for a US practice that may be inferior for the purpose of analysis. For example, although many large UK companies revalue fixed assets occasionally, annual revaluation is far from standard and is very difficult for an analyst to simulate; therefore, it may be necessary to stick to historical cost.

Bearing these factors in mind, and sifting the contents of previous chapters for items that would affect earnings and net assets, the benchmark in Table 26 emerges.

When trying to cope with European comparisons, greater problems

TABLE 27.	ADJUSTMENTS FOR EUROPEAN COMPANIES TO UK BENCHMARK
Conservatism	Increase net asset values
Historical cost	Increase net asset values
LIFO	Increase inventory values for some
Translation	Extract translation adjustments from German and other users of the temporal method
Consolidation	Beware lack of consolidation
Associated companies	Increase net assets and profit in cases of non-use of equity method
Leases	Increase fixed assets and liabilities where leases are not capitalised
Pensions	Examine carefully: extract any pension provisions from shareholders' funds
Provisions	Increase shareholders' funds by portion of general provisions
Tax	Decrease depreciation where caused by tax

arise. In the case of Germany, the Association of Investment Analysts (Deutsche Vereinigung für Finanzanalyse und Anlageberatung: DVFA) tries to adjust for the discretionary items in German accounts. Its objective is particularly to adjust earnings, not to a UK benchmark of course, but to a more comparable German basis. The rules were rearranged in 1987 as a result of the implementation of the Fourth and Seventh Directives. Some of the main adjustments to German published net profit figures are:

- Exclusion of all extraordinary and prior-year items (even gains and losses on the sale of fixed assets, which would be 'exceptional items' in the UK)
- Elimination of excess depreciation due to tax rules or for other reasons
- Removal of the effects of changes to long-term provisions, which are largely discretionary
- Elimination of currency gains and losses on non-trading activities.

Our task is to go beyond national comparisons. We need to take account of the major differences examined in Chapters IV to VIII. A reminder of those differences is the classification of countries in Chapter III (Figure 1). All European countries except for the UK, Ireland, Denmark and The Netherlands are in the macro group. For accounts from these countries, some of the adjustments in Table 27 may be necessary.

In more detail, the benchmark towards which one might wish to work for international purposes could have the features shown in Table 28. Of these various adjustments, some will be simple to obtain from published accounts and some will be capable of estimation. However, some

---

TABLE 28.   BENCHMARK FOR INTERNATIONAL COMPARISON OF EARNINGS AND NET ASSETS

Earnings

1. After depreciation, interest, tax, minority profits and preference dividend
2. Excluding extraordinary items
3. Historical cost numbers
4. Provisions for risks or contingencies not charged against profit
5. Tax-based provisions and depreciation not charged
6. All subsidiaries included
7. Excluding differences on translation of foreign financial statements, but including exchange differences on transactions, loans etc.
8. Excluding amortisation of goodwill
9. Including share of profits of associated companies (20–50%)
10. Excluding depreciation of set-up costs which should be charged in one year
11. Interest expenses not capitalised
12. Deferred tax not accounted for, except when expected to be paid soon

Net assets

1. Standardise on historical cost for most assets but, if possible, current value of property
2. FIFO not LIFO
3. Exclude capitalised goodwill, set-up costs, interest
4. Deferred tax treated as reserve unless expected to be paid soon, when it is a provision
5. Minorities included
6. All subsidiaries included
7. Closing rate translation
8. Associates treated by equity method
9. Tax-based provisions and those for risks or contingencies treated as reserves
10. Leases capitalised

---

problems will not be solvable from published information, although analysts may find that the list in Table 28 raises useful questions to be asked at meetings with companies.

In summary, it is likely to remain impossible for many years to achieve precise international comparisons of earnings and net assets figures. However, this does not mean that users of financial statements should just give up and pretend that all companies are using the same rules. Approximate adjustments and informed questions will lead to better decision-making. Experts will be better at it than amateurs.

MULTILINGUAL GLOSSARY OF ACCOUNTING TERMS

The language difficulties involved in international financial analysis were discussed in Chapter I and specifically for the UK and the US in Chapter II. This glossary examines a number of common accounting terms, discussing their meanings to UK and US accountants. The equivalents in French (F), German (G), Dutch (NL), Spanish (E) and Italian (I) are given. In cases where the meaning is obvious (e.g. 'bank', 'wages'), only the translations are given.

Cross-references within the glossary are shown in italic type.

Account   A record of all the bookkeeping entries relating to a particular item. For example, the wages account would record all the payments of wages. An account in the double-entry system has a debit side (left) and a credit side (right). Often accounts are referred to as T-accounts, because of the rulings on the page that divide the left from the right and underline the title. Of course, pages have now generally been replaced by spaces on a computer disk. A business may have thousands of accounts, including one for each *debtor* and *creditor.*

In the early days of accounting, there were only personal accounts (for people who owed and were owed money). Later, there were 'real' accounts for property of various sorts; and 'nominal' accounts for impersonal, unreal items like wages and electricity. Accounts may be collected together in groups in ledgers or books of account.

In the UK, 'accounts' may also mean financial statements, such as *balance sheets* and *profit and loss accounts. F: poste G: Konto NL: post E: cuenta I: conto*

Accountancy and accounting   These terms are used interchangeably by many people. However, in the UK it tends to be, for example, the **accountancy** profession, but management **accounting**. That is, the former tends to be associated with the profession, and the latter with the subject matter, particularly in the context of education or theory. In the US, the word 'accountancy' is rarer.   *F: comptabilité G: Buchführung NL: verslaggeving E: contabilidad I: contabilità*

Accounts payable   US expression for *creditors* in the UK. These are amounts owed by the business, usually as a result of purchases in the normal course of trade from suppliers who allow the business to pay at some point after purchase. Discounts will often be allowed for early payment of such accounts. The total of accounts payable at the period

138

end form part of current liabilities on a balance sheet. See **Creditor** for translations

Accounts receivable   US expression for *debtors* in the UK. These are the amounts to be paid to the business by outsiders, normally as a result of sales to customers who have not yet settled their bills. Accounts receivable are valued at the amount of the accounts, less an allowance ('provision' in UK terminology) for any amounts thought likely to be uncollectable. Those which are fairly certain to be uncollectable are bad debts; and there may also be allowances for specific amounts expected to be uncollectable, and general allowances against the total of accounts receivable. The general allowances would be calculated in the light of past experience with bad debts. All these allowances reflect the perceived need for conservatism, particularly in the valuation of such current assets. After taking into account all these provisions, the total of accounts receivable will be part of current assets on a balance sheet. See **Debtor** for translations

Accruals   In the case of expenses, those which relate to a year but will not be paid until the following year. They result from the need regularly to draw up financial statements at a fixed time (for example, at the end of a company's year).

   During a year, electricity will be used or properties will be rented, yet at the year end the related bills may not have been paid. Thus, at the year end, 'accrued' expenses are charged against income by accountants even though cash has not been paid, nor perhaps the bills even received. The double entry for this is the creation of a current liability on the balance sheets. This practice may apply also to wages and salaries, taxes and so on. An allocation of amounts to 'this year' and 'next year' may be necessary where a supplier's account straddles two accounting years. The practice is an example of the use of the matching concept.

   Similarly, some accounts of suppliers which are paid in any year may be wholly or partly paid on behalf of the activities of the next year. In this case, the relevant expenses for the year will have to be adjusted downwards by the accountant, and a current asset called 'prepayments' recorded on the balance sheet. Thus, payments of property taxes and insurance premiums may be partly prepayments.   *F: comptes de régularisation G: Rechnungsabgrenzungsposten NL: te belaten kosten E: ajustes por periodificación I: accantonamenti*

Allowances   US expression for *provisions*, i.e. amounts charged against profit in anticipation of reductions in value. See **Provisions** for translations

Amortisation   A word used, particularly in North America, to refer to *depreciation* of intangible assets. See **Depreciation** for translations

Annual general meeting (AGM)   In the UK, the meeting at which shareholders may question directors on the contents of the annual report and financial statements; vote on the directors' recommendation for dividends; vote on replacements for retiring members of the board; and conduct other business within the association. The AGM of a company is held once a year; to be more exact, under UK law there must be a gap of no more than 18 months between AGMs.

The equivalent US expression is 'annual meeting of stockholders'. *F: assemblée générale ordinaire G: ordentliche Hauptversammlung NL: algemene vergadering van aandeelhouders E: junta general I: assemblea annuale degli azionisti*

Annual report   A document sent to shareholders after a company's year end. It contains a report by the president or chairman of the board, a review of the year or report by directors, the financial statements and notes, and the report of auditors.

The report of the chairman (UK) or president (US) is usually couched in fairly vague, non-numerical terms. It outlines the progress and problems of the year, and looks forward to the opportunities of the future. It tends to thank the staff and customers, and possibly to make a political point or two.

The directors' report (UK) or review of the year (US) contains much more detailed financial information. *F: rapport annuel G: Geschäftsbericht NL: jaarverslag E: memoria anual I: rapporto annuale*

Articles of association   A document drawn up at the foundation of a UK company, setting out the rights and duties of the shareholders and directors, and the relationship between one class of shareholders and another (see also *memorandum*). In the US, similar rules will be found in the *bylaws*   *F: statuts G: Gesellshaftsvertrag NL: statuten E: estatutos I: statuti*

Assets   Generally, things owned that have future economic benefits. However, it turns out that to define exactly what an accountant means by an 'asset' is exceptionally difficult. Various attempts have been made, particularly in the US. A definition is contained in part of the conceptual framework project in the US (in Statement of Financial Accounting Concepts no. 3). According to that document, the existence of an asset relies upon 'probable future economic benefits obtained or controlled by a particular entity as a result of past transactions or events'.   *F: éléments de l'actif G: Vermögensgegenstanden NL: activa E: activo I: attività*

Associated company   A British term for a company over which another has significant influence. The term is not so well known in the US. In both countries, the equity method is used for such companies. A company will be presumed to be an associated company if it is owned to the extent of 20% to 50%. Above 50% ownership it becomes a subsidiary; under 20% ownership it becomes a trade investment (see '*consolidated*'). Companies held as joint ventures with other owners will be treated as associated companies.   *F: participation G: Beteiligungsgesellschaft NL: minderheidsdeelneming E: compañia asociada I: consociata*

Audit   The basic aim of a modern audit in the UK or the US is to give an opinion on whether the financial statements drawn up by the directors of a company give a fair presentation in accordance with GAAP (US) or a true and fair view (UK). In order to do this an auditor needs to check the physical existence and valuation of important assets; and he needs to examine the systems of internal control to ensure that transactions are likely to have been recorded correctly.

If internal control is poor he will ask for it to be improved and he will increase the amount of checking done on sample transactions. If the control systems look good, relatively small samples of various types of transactions may be checked.

The auditor would generally be expected to circularise a sample of some of the debtors to confirm that they exist. He would normally attend the count of the inventory (in the UK, the annual stock take). He would try to spot and to question unusual items in the books of account or financial statements. The rules for auditing vary from firm to firm, but are to some extent found in auditing standards.   *F: révision G: Prüfung NL: accountantscontrole E: auditoría I: revisione contabile*

Auditor   *F: commissaire aux comptes G: Wirtschaftsprüfer NL: registeraccountant E: auditor I: revisore, sindaco*

Authorised share capital   The maximum amount of a particular type of share in a particular company that may be issued. The amount is laid down in the company's *memorandum* (UK) or certificate of incorporation (US). It may be interesting information to shareholders as it puts a limit on the number of co-owners. The memorandum can be varied by a sufficient majority of the shareholders.   *F: (no direct equivalent) G: genehmigtes Kapital NL: maatschappelijk kapitaal E: capital autorizado I: capitale approvato*

Balance sheet   A snap-shot of the accounting records of assets, liabilities and capital of a business at a particular moment, most obviously the accounting year end. The balance sheet is the longest established of the main financial statements produced by a business. As its name suggests, it is a sheet of the balances from the double-entry system at a particular time. It is important to note that it is probably not a snap-shot of what the business is **worth**. This is because not all the business's items of value are recognised by accountants as assets, and because the asset valuation methods used are normally based on past costs rather than on present market values.   *F: bilan G: Bilanz NL: balans E: balance I: stato patrimoniale*

Bank   *F: banque G: Bank NL: bank E: banco I: Banca*

Bearer share   Shares (of public companies) that are not registered. The shares pass by delivery, not by registration. These are not found in English legal system countries, e.g. the UK and the USA.   *F: action au porteur G: Inhaber Aktie NL: aandeel aan toonder E: acción al portador I: azioni al portatore*

Board of directors (management)   *F: directoire G: Vorstand NL: raad van bestuur E: consejo de administración I: consiglio d'amministrazione*

Bonus issue   The UK expression for the issue of more free shares to the existing shareholders. The retained profits are capitalised. The US equivalents are *stock dividend* and *stock split*.   *F: bonus G: Bonus-gewährung NL: agio bonus E: acciones liberadas I: compenso*

Bylaws   The rules of a US corporation concerning the relationships between and among the board of directors and the different classes of shareholders. The bylaws need to be registered with the appropriate state authorities, with the certificate of incorporation, before a corporation can be properly born. In the UK the equivalent documents are the *articles of association* and the *memorandum*. See **Articles of association** for translation.

Capital allowances   A system of *depreciation* used in the determination of taxable income that is unique to the British Isles. The rates are specified in annual Finance Acts; they tend to be more generous than the depreciation that accountants would charge for financial accounting purposes. *No direct equivalents*

Cash flow   Sometimes used to refer very loosely to the amount of cash coming into or going out of a business in a particular period. However, it can be used as a more precise accounting term, particularly in North America, to refer to net income with depreciation charges added back. The latter will have been deducted in the calculation of the former, but are not of course a cash payment of the period in question. Thus, profit plus depreciation gives an impression of cash generated by trading operations. This is not very exact, particularly because of changes in inventory (stocks) and because of outstanding credit sales and purchases which have been included in the calculation of profit but will not yet have led to cash movements. However, as a quick measure it may have its uses.

In statements of cash flows (US) or source and application of funds statements (UK), the 'cash flow' is an important opening figure.
F: cash flow, autofinancement G: Cashflow, Finanzfluss NL: cash flow E: cash flow I: cash flow

Common stock   US term for the *ordinary shares* in a corporation. Normally a majority of the ownership capital will comprise issues of common stock, though *preferred stock* is also issued. Stock usually has a par value. The amount that would have to be paid for one share will be determined, in the case of a listed share, by the daily price on the stock exchange. The total of common stock is part of the shareholders' equity of a company.

Consolidated   Statements presenting the position and results of a parent and its subsidiary companies as if they were a single entity. Consolidation ignores the separation of parents and subsidiaries due to legal and geographical factors; it accounts for the group of companies as a single entity. Approximately, the financial statements of all the companies in the group are added together, with adjustments to extract intra-group trading and indebtedness.   *F: consolidé G: konsolidiert NL: geconsolideerd E: consolidado I: consolidato*

Contingent   For example, possible future liabilities. As part of conservatism, accountants recognise all reasonable probable losses in advance. However, some losses are merely 'possible' and are contingent upon some event, like the loss of a law case or a debtor defaulting on a bill of exchange which the company has guaranteed. These 'contingencies' are not accounted for, in the sense of adjusting the financial statements, but are added to the notes to the balance sheet. A suitable note will explain the cause of the contingency and, at least in the UK, give the amount (or an estimate). Instructions on practice are contained in accounting standards: SSAP 18 in the UK and SFAS 5 in the US.

F: éventuel G: eventuell NL: eventueel E: contingencia I: contingente

Creditor   A creditor is a 'truster', someone to whom a business owes money. The US expression is '*accounts payable*'. Creditors are created by purchases 'on credit' or loans of various sorts. Short-term creditors are included under 'current liabilities' on a balance sheet; they are expected to be paid within the year. If credit purchases are the cause, the title used might be 'trade creditors'.

Long-term creditors are those who are not expected to be paid within the year. These might be trade creditors but would more likely be holders of bonds or debentures. The latter would normally be entitled to receive interest, whereas trade creditors are not. However, trade creditors often offer discounts for prompt payment, which is an implied way of charging interest.

Creditors of all sorts are shown in a balance sheet at the amounts which a business expects to pay. Particularly in the case of long-term loans, this may be different from the amount originally borrowed or from the amount that would have to be paid to redeem the loan at the balance sheet date.   *F: créancier G: Gläubiger NL: crediteur E: acreedor I: fornitore*

Current assets   By convention, an asset on a balance sheet is 'current' if it is expected to change its form within a year from the balance sheet date. Such assets include inventories (stocks), accounts receivable (US) or debtors (UK), and cash. Also, a balance sheet may include current asset investments; that is, those designed to be held for a short period. The 'one-year' convention is a rule of thumb for the more fundamental distinction between those assets that are to continue to be used in the business (*fixed assets* in the UK) and assets that are part of circulating or trading capital. Thus, just as investments can be fixed or current assets, so automobiles can be fixed (if part of a fleet of company cars) or current (if part of the trading inventory of a car dealer) assets. *F: actif circulant G: Umlaufvermögen NL: vlottende middelen E: activo circulante I: attività corrente*

Current liabilities   Those amounts on a balance sheet that are expected to be paid by the business within a year. Thus they will include trade creditors (UK) or accounts payable (US), certain tax liabilities, and proposed dividends. Bank overdrafts are included on the grounds that they fluctuate in size and are technically recallable at short notice.

Current liabilities are valued at their 'face value', the amount that is expected to be paid.   *F: dettes à court terme G: kurzfristige Verbindlichkeiten NL: schulden op korte termijn E: pasivo circulante I: passività corrente*

Debtor   In a balance sheet, debtors are usually mostly trade debtors, i.e. customers who have not yet paid cash. The US terminology is '*accounts receivable*'. Such amounts are shown as current assets because they are generally expected to be paid within the year.

In a balance sheet, debtors are valued at what they are expected to pay, bearing in mind the principle of conservatism. Thus, bad debts are written off, and provisions (allowances in US terminology) are made for doubtful debts. The provisions can be both specific (against suspected debts) and general (based on the average experience of bad debts). *F: débiteur G: Schuldner NL: debiteur E: duedor I: crediti*

Deferred tax   Caused by timing differences between when an amount is recognised for accounting income purposes and when it is recognised for taxable income. For example, suppose that depreciation for tax purposes (i.e. in the UK, capital allowances) is more rapid than for accounting purposes; in such a case, in the early years of an asset's life, tax depreciation will be larger than accounting depreciation (and vice versa later). Thus there are timing differences. *F: impôt différé G: latente Steuern NL: latente belastingverplichtinge E: impuestos diferidos I: imposte differite*

Depreciation   A charge against the profit of a period to represent the wearing out of fixed assets in that period. So, machinery and equipment, vehicles and buildings are depreciated though land normally is not. The technique of depreciation means that accountants do not charge the whole cost of a fixed asset against the profit of the year of purchase, but they charge it gradually over the years of the use and wearing out of the asset. This fits with the matching concept. *F: dotation aux comptes d'amortissements G: Abschreibung NL: af-schrijving E: depreciación I: ammortamento*

Discount   *F: prime de remboursement G: Disagio NL: disagio E: descu-ento I: sconto*

Dividend   *F: dividende G: Dividende NL: dividend E: dividendo I: divi-dendo*

Doubtful debts   Specifically or generally identified amounts of debts considered likely to become bad. Provisions for bad debts are charged in advance. *F: créances douteuses G: Zweifelhafte Forderungen NL: dubieuze debiteuren E: deudores morosos I: credito dubbio*

Exceptional   A UK expression for those items in a profit and loss account that are within the normal activities of the business, but are of unusual size. The treatment for these, as laid down in accounting standards (SSAP 6), is to disclose them separately in the account or the notes to it. Such items are to be distinguished from *extraordinary* items. *F: exceptionnel G: ausserordentlich NL: buitengewoon E: estraordinario I: straordinario*

Expenses   Payments for goods and services that relate to the earning of profit in the current year.   *F: charges G: Aufwendung NL: uitgaven E: gastos I: spese*

Extraordinary   Gains or losses which are outside the normal activities of the business, are of significant size, and are not expected to recur. The rules for extraordinary items are to be found in accounting standards: SSAP 6 in the UK, and APB Opinion 30 in the US. Such items are to be distinguished from *exceptional* items.   *F: exceptionnel G: ausser-ordentlich NL: buitengewoon E: estraordinario I: straordinario*

FIFO: first in, first out   A common assumption for accounting purposes about the flow of items of raw materials or other *inventories (stocks)*. It need not be expected to correspond with physical reality, but may be taken for accounting purposes. The assumption is that the first units to be received as part of inventories are the first ones to be used up or sold. This means that the most recent units are deemed to be those left at the period end. When prices are rising, and assuming a reasonably constant purchasing of materials, FIFO leads to a fairly up-to-date closing inventory figure. However, it gives an out-of-date and therefore low figure for the cost of sales. This leads to what many argue is an overstatement of profit figures, when prices are rising. In order to correct for this for **tax** purposes, in the UK a special stock relief was allowed until 1984, and in the US the use of *LIFO* has been allowed. *Same initials used internationally.*

Finished goods   *F: produits finis G: Fertigerzeugnisse NL: gereed produkt E: productos terminados I: prodotti finiti*

Fixed assets   Mainly a UK, rather than a US, expression, meaning the assets that are to continue to be used in the business, such as land, buildings and machines. The opposite is *current assets*, which would be traded and expected to change their form within a year from the balance sheet date, as cash or inventories (stock) do. An equivalent US expression is 'property, plant and equipment'.   *F: immobilisations G: Sachanlagen NL: vaste activa E: activo fijo I: immobili*

Gearing   A measure of the degree to which a business is funded by loans rather than shareholders' equity. The US expression is *'leverage'.* *F: ratio d'endettement G: Kapitalintensität NL: gearing E: not used I: gearing*

General reserve   Amounts of undistributed profit that are available for distribution to shareholders.   *F: réserve facultative G: Pauschalwertberichtigung NL: algemene reserve E: reserva voluntaria I: ríserva disponibile*

Goodwill   In the US and the UK, the amount paid for a business in excess of the fair value of its net assets at the date of acquisition. It exists because a going concern business is usually worth more than the sum of the values of its separable net assets. This may be looked upon as its ability to earn future profits above those of a similar newly formed company or it may be seen as the 'goodwill' of customers, the established network of contacts, loyal staff and skilled management. *F: fonds de commerce, survaleur G: Firmenwert, Geschäftswert NL: goodwill E: fondo de comercio I: avviamento*

Group   *F: groupe G: Konzern NL: concern E: grupo I: gruppo*

Hire   *F: louer G: mieten NL: huren E: alquilar I: noleggiare*

Holding company   A company that owns or controls others. In the narrow use of the expression, it implies that the company does not actively trade but operates through various subsidiaries. The accounting treatment for such parent–subsidiary relationships is to prepare consolidated financial statements for the combined group.   *F: sociétémère G: Muttergesellschaft NL: holding E: matriz I: casa madre*

Income statement   The most common US name for the statement of revenues and expenses of a particular period, leading to the calculation of net income or net profit. For companies registered with the Securities and Exchange Commission a full annual income statement must be published, and quarterly information must also be published. The income statement shows the annual sales and other revenues, and then the expenses or costs of manufacture, administration, marketing, interest and taxation.

The income statement is in either vertical/statement or horizontal/two-sided/account format.

See the equivalent UK term **Profit and loss account**, for translations.

Income tax   The income of all forms of business in the US is subject to income tax. In the UK, the owners of unincorporated businesses pay income tax, but companies pay corporation tax. *F: impôt sur le bénéfice G: Einkommensteuer NL: inkomstenbelasting E: impuesto sobre la renta I: imposta sul reddito*

Indirect costs   Costs that are not specifically identified with particular units of output. *F: frais indirects G: indirekte Kosten NL: indirekte kosten E: costes indirectos I: costi indiretti*

Intangible assets   Assets that are not physical or tangible, such as *goodwill* or *patents*. *F: immobilisations incorporelles G: immaterielle Wirtschaftsgüter NL: imateriele activa E: intangibles I: intangibili*

Interim dividend   *F: acomptes sur dividendes G: Vorabdividende NL: interim-dividend E: dividendo activo a cuenta I: acconto dividendo*

Interim report   The UK expression for a half-yearly report for companies listed on the Stock Exchange.

In the US, quarterly interim reports are required from companies registered with the Securities and Exchange Commission. *F: rapport intérimaire G: Zwischenbericht NL: tussentijds verslag E: informe interino I: rapporto semestrale*

Inventories   Raw materials, work-in-progress and goods ready for sale. In the UK, the word 'stocks' is generally used instead. See **Stocks** for translations.

Leverage   US term for the degree to which a business is funded by loans rather than by shareholders' equity. In a highly levered company, a percentage increase in trading profit will be magnified by the time it reaches the stockholders, because the return to the lenders is a fixed amount of interest.

See the equivalent UK expression, **Gearing**, for translations.

Liabilities   Amounts of money that must be paid by a business at some future date. Most liabilities are of known amount and date. They include long-term loans, bank overdrafts and amounts owed to suppliers. There are current and non-current liabilities. The former are expected to be paid within a year from the date of the balance sheet on which they appear. Most measures of liquidity include knowing the total of current liabilities; net current assets is the difference between the current assets and the current liabilities.

Liabilities are valued at the amounts expected to be paid at the expected maturity date. In some cases, amounts that are not quite certain will be included as liabilities; they will be valued at the best estimate available. The convention of conservatism suggests that amounts that are reasonably likely to be liabilities should be treated thus. Less likely amounts are called *contingencies*. *F: dettes G: Verbindlichkeiten NL: schulden E: deudas I: passività*

LIFO: last in, first out   One of the methods available for the calculation of the cost of *inventories* (*stocks*), in those frequent cases where it is difficult or impossible to determine exactly which items remain or have been used. When prices are rising, LIFO will lead to more up-to-date values for the use of inventory in cost of sales and thus lower profits. Therefore it is popular with many companies in the US, where it is allowed for tax purposes (as long as it is also used for financial statements).

However, the inventory value shown in the balance sheet may be seriously misleading as it will be based on very old prices. Thus the method is discouraged by the appropriate accounting standard (SSAP 9) in the UK, and is rarely found there: *FIFO* is preferred. *Same initials used internationally*

Memorandum   A legal document drawn up as part of the registration of a company in the UK. It includes a record of the company's name, its registered office, its purposes and its authorised share capital. The other document drawn up at the birth of a UK company is the *articles of association*. In the US, the equivalent document to the memorandum has several names, including the certificate of incorporation. See **Articles of association** for translations.

Merger   Normally a business combination that is agreed by all parties.   *F: fusion G: Verschmelzung NL: fusie E: fusión I: fusione*

Minority interests   The capital provided by, and earned for, group shareholders who are not parent company shareholders. Many subsidiary companies are not fully owned by the parent company. This means that they are partly owned by 'minority' shareholders outside the group. In the preparation of consolidated financial statements, accountants bring in 100% of all assets, liabilities, expenses and revenues of subsidiaries. This is because the group fully **controls** the subsidiary, even if it does not fully own it. In such financial statements, the subsidiary is submerged into the rest of the group, and the capital provided by the minority shareholders is separately recognised as part of the capital of the group called 'minority interests'. This amount grows each time the relevant subsidiary makes a profit that is not distributed.

In the consolidated profit and loss account, the share of the group profit owned by minorities is also shown as 'profit attributable to minorities'. *F: intérêts minoritaires G: Anteile im Fremdbesitz NL: minderheidsbelang E: interes minoritario I: minoranza*

Net current assets   The net current assets or *working capital* of a business is the excess of the current assets (like cash, inventories and debtors or accounts receivable) over the current liabilities (like trade creditors and overdrafts). This is a measure of the extent to which the business is safe from liquidity problems. However, the movement of the total from year to year, or the current ratio (of current assets to current liabilities), might be more useful information. See **Working capital** for translations.

Ordinary share   The US term is *common stock.   F: action G: Stammaktie NL: gewoon aandeel E: acción ordinaria I: azione*
Overheads   Costs that are not identified with particular units of output.   *F: frais généraux G: Gemeinkosten NL: algemene kosten E: gastos generales I: spese generali*

Paid-in surplus   US expression for part of the amounts of money paid by investors when they purchased a company's shares. Most shares in the US have a par value. Usually shares are issued at above par value, in which case the capital paid in is divided into share capital (at par) and paid-in surplus (the excess above par). For most analytical purposes, paid-in surplus is treated exactly as if it were 'share capital'.

There are several alternative titles for these amounts, including 'paid-in capital'. See the equivalent UK term, **Share premium** for translations.
Partnership   *F: société en nom collectif G: offene Handelsgesellschaft NL: maatschap E: sociedad comanditaria I: società in nome collettivo*
Patent   *F: brevet G: Patent NL: octrooi E: patente I: brevetto*
Pension fund   *F: caisse de retraite G: Pensionkasse NL: pensioenfonds E: fondo de pensiones I: fondo pensione*
Plant   *F: matériel G: Maschinen NL: installaties E: instalaciónes I: impianti e macchinare*
Preferred stock, preference shares   A minority of shares in some companies are issued as preference shares (UK) or preferred stock (US). These shares normally have preference over *ordinary shares* or

common stock for dividend payments and for the return of capital if a company is wound up. That is, ordinary/common dividends cannot be paid in a particular year until the preference/preferred dividend (generally including any arrears), which is usually a fixed percentage, has been paid.   *F: actions préférentielles G: Vorzugsaktien NL: preferente aandelen E: acciones preferentes I: azioni privilegiate*

Preliminary expenses   The expenses of setting up a business.   *F: frais d'établissement   G: Gründungskosten   NL: voorbereidingskosten E: gastos de establicimiento I: spese preliminare*

Price/earnings ratio   The ratio of the price of an ordinary share to the most recent annual earnings attributable to one share.   *F: rapport cours/bénéfice G: Kurs/Gewinn Verhältnis NL: koers/winstverhouding E: price/earnings ratio I: prezzo utile*

Prior period   *F: exercice antérieur G: Vorjahr NL: voorafgaande periode E: ejercicio anterior I: ultimo esercizio*

Private limited company   *F: société à responsibilité limitée G: Gesellschaft mit beschränkter Haftung NL: besloten vennootschap E: sociedad de responsibilidad limitada I: società a responsabilità limitata*

Profit and loss account   The UK expression for the financial statement that summarises the difference between the revenues and expenses of a period. Such statements may be drawn up frequently for the managers of a business, but a full audited statement is normally only published for each accounting year. The equivalent US expression is *'income statement'*.   *F: compte de résultat G: Gewinn- und Verlustrechnung NL: winst- en verliesrekening E: cuenta de pérdidad y ganancias I: conto perdite e profitti*

Provisions   Unfortunately, there is some vagueness about the use of the words 'provisions' and *'reserves'*. However, a provision in the UK usually means an amount charged against profit to reduce the recorded value of an asset or to cover an expected liability, even if the exact amount or timing of the liability is uncertain. A reserve, on the other hand, is an amount voluntarily or compulsorily set aside out of profit (after it has been calculated), often in order to demonstrate that the amount is not to be distributed as dividends.

However, US usage of the words is loose. For example, it is not unknown for accountants and others to talk about a 'bad debt reserve'; and in some continental European countries there may be very large 'provisions for contingencies' that Anglo-Saxon practice would treat as reserves. In US terminology, *'allowance'* is often used instead of 'provision', and an amount set aside to cover an expected liability would usually be called a reserve.   *F: provision G: Rückstellung NL: voorziening E: provisión I: fondo*

Proxy   *F: formule de procuration G: Stellvertretung NL: volmacht E: poder I: per procura*

Public company   A company whose securities (shares and loan stock) may be publicly traded. In the UK, the legal form of such a company is set out in the Companies Acts. The company must have 'public limited company' (or PLC) as part of its name. There are equivalents to this form in other European countries, but in the US the nearest equivalent is a corporation that is registered with the Securities and Exchange Commission.   *F: société anonyme G: Aktiengesellschaft NL: naamloze vennootschap E: sociedad anónima I: società per azioni*

Quoted   *F: admis à la cote officielle G: an einer Börse notiert NL: genoteerd E: cotizado I: quotato*

Realisable value   The money that could be obtained by selling an asset.   *F: valeur de réalisation G: Börsen- oder Marktpreis NL: opbrengstwaarde E: valor de realización I: valore realizzabile*

Receivables   The US expression for amounts of money due to a business; often known as 'accounts receivable'. See the UK term **Debtors** for translations.

Reducing balance   A technique of calculating the *depreciation* charge, usually for machines, whereby the annual charge reduces over the years of an asset's life. A fixed percentage depreciation is charged each year on the cost (first year) or the undepreciated cost (subsequent years).   *F: dégressif G: degressive NL: degressief E: degresiva I: not used*

Research and development   *F: recherche et développement G: Forschung und Entwicklung NL: onderzoek en ontwikkeling E: investigaciones y desarrollo I: ricerche e sviluppi*

Reserves   UK term for amounts notionally set aside out of profits (after the latter have been calculated), often to register the fact that they are voluntarily or compulsorily undistributable. The US equivalent is an appropriation of retained earnings. Reserves should be distinguished from *provisions*. In the UK, the latter are charged in the calculation of profit, and represent reductions in the value of assets or anticipations of future liabilities. Of course, neither reserves nor provisions are amounts of cash. A provision is an accounting expense, and a reserve is an accounting allocation of undistributed profit from one heading to another. Reserves belong to shareholders and are part of a total of shareholders' equity, which also includes share capital. This total is represented by all the assets of the business, less the liabilities owed to outsiders.

It should be noted that this terminology is used somewhat loosely by some accountants. In the US, 'reserve' is used to cover some of the meanings of 'provision' in the UK.   *F: réserve G: Rücklage NL: reserve E: riserva I: riserva*

Retained profit, retained earnings   Amounts of profit, earned in the preceding year and former years, that have not yet been paid out as dividends. 'Retained earnings' is a typical US expression for such amounts, though it would also be understood in the UK. 'Retained profit' is a more usual UK expression.   *F: report à nouveau; free reserves G: Rücklagen; Gewinnvortrag NL: ingehouden winsten E: beneficios retenidos I: utili non distribuiti*

Revaluation   Conventional accounting uses historical cost as the basis for the valuation of assets. However, in some countries, including the UK but not the US, it is acceptable to revalue fixed assets, either annually or from time to time. These revaluations can be done on the basis of current replacement cost or net realisable value. It is quite normal for large UK companies to show land and buildings at revalued amounts in their balance sheets. Clearly, the purpose of this is to avoid a seriously misleading impression of their worth, when prices have risen substantially.   *F: réévaluation G: Zuschreibung NL: herwaardering E: revaluación I: rivalutazione*

Sales   The figure for sales recorded in the financial statements for a period will include all those sales agreed or delivered in the period, rather than those that are paid for in cash. The sales figure will be shown net of sales taxes (VAT in the UK).

In the UK, the word '*turnover*' is used in the financial statements, although 'sales' is generally used in the books of account. See **Turnover** for translations.

Shareholders' funds   The total of the shareholders' interest in a company. This will include the original share capital, amounts contributed in excess of the par value of shares (i.e. share premium or paid-in surplus), and retained profits. In the US, this total is sometimes called *stockholders' equity*. *F: fonds propres G: Eigenkapital NL: eigen vermogen E: fondos proprios I: patrimonio netto*

Share premium   Amounts paid into a company (by shareholders when they purchased shares from the company) in excess of the nominal value of the shares. The nominal value is little more than a label for the shares, but all UK shares have such a value. Shares are recorded at nominal values. However, share premium may be treated for most purposes exactly as if it were share capital. Both are included in shareholders' equity.

In the US there are many equivalent expressions, e.g. *paid-in-surplus*.   *F: prime d'émission G: Kapitalzuzahung NL: agioreserve E: prima de emisión I: fondo sovraprezza azione*

Stock dividend, stock split   US terms to describe the issue of free extra shares to existing shareholders, combined with the capitalisation of retained earnings. A stock dividend is an extra issue of up to about 25% of the number of existing shares. A stock split is an extra issue, usually of over about 20%. The two issues are accounted for differently.

The UK equivalent expressions are *bonus issue*, scrip issue and capitalisation issue.

Stockholders' equity   US expression for the total stake in a company owned by the stockholders, including their invested capital and retained earnings. A more detailed entry may be found under *shareholders' funds*, which is an expression also used in the US, and more readily understood in the UK.

Stocks   Raw materials, work-in-progress and finished goods; also known as *inventories*.

The term 'stocks' is also used in the US for securities of various kinds; for example, *common stock* or *preferred stock* (equivalent to ordinary and preference shares in UK terminology). However, the word 'share' is also understood in the US, so that 'stockholder' and 'shareholder' are interchangeable. In the UK this meaning survives, particularly in the expressions 'stock exchange' and 'loan stock'.   *F: valeurs d'exploitation G: Vorräte NL: voorraden E: existencias I: inventario*

Straight line   A system of calculating the annual *depreciation* expense of a fixed asset. This method charges equal annual instalments against profit over the useful life of the asset. In total, the cost of the asset less any estimated residual scrap value is depreciated. This method is simple to use and thus very popular.   *F: linéaire G: linear NL: linear E: de línea recta I: a quote costanti*

Subsidiary   *F: filiale G: Tochtergesellschaft NL: dochtermaatschappij E: subsidiaria I: società controllata*

Takeover   Normally a business combination where one party is clearly buying the other.   *F: offre publique d'achat G: Erwerb durch Aktienübernahme NL: overname E: OPA I: scalata*

Tax   *F: impôt G: Steuer NL: belasting E: impuesto I: imposta*

Trade mark   *F: brevet G: Warenzeichen NL: handelsmerk E: marca I: marchio di fabbrica*

Trading profit   The excess of the turnover over cost of sales.   *F: marge commerciale G: Betriebsergebnis NL: bedrijfsresultaat E: resultado operativo I: utile operative*

Translation (currency)   *F: conversion G: Umrechnung NL: valutaomrekening E: conversión I: traduzione*

True and fair view   The overriding legal requirement for the presentation of financial statements of companies in the UK and most of the

Commonwealth. The nearest US equivalent is 'fair presentation'. *F: image fidèle G: ein den tatsächlichen Verhältnissen entsprechendes Bild NL: getrouw beeld E: imagen fiel I: quadro fedele*

Turnover   The UK expression used in profit and loss accounts for the *sales* revenue of an accounting period. This is shown net of value-added tax.   *F: chiffre d'affaires G: Umsatz NL: omzet E: ventas I: fatturato*

Unusual items   US term for amounts that are not outside the ordinary course of the business, but are unusual in size or incidence. The approximate UK equivalent is *exceptional* items. See **Exceptional** for translations.

Valuation   *F: évaluation G: Bewertung NL: waardering E: valoración I: valutazione*

Value added tax   *F: taxe sur la valeur ajoutée G: Umsatzsteuer NL: belasting op toegevoegde waarde E: impuesto sobre el valor añadido I: imposta sul valore aggiunto*

Wages   *F: salaires G: Löhne NL: lonen E: salarios I: salari*

Working capital   The difference between current assets and current liabilities. This total is also known as *net current assets*, under which entry there are more details.   *F: fonds de roulement G: Betriebsmittel NL: werkkapitaal E: capital trabajo I: capitale circolante*

Work-in-progress   *F: produits en cours G: unfertige Erzeugnisse NL: onderhanden werk E: productos en curso I: lavoro in corso*

COUNTRIES AT A GLANCE

The following pages show some important accounting features of eleven major commercial countries. The features are in the same order for all of the countries. Readers should note that the great degree of abbreviation necessary here may cause some information to be misleading in certain circumstances. Reference should be made to the detail given earlier in this book, and to other works of reference.

AUSTRALIA

Feature	Practice
Law	English
Main rule-makers	Company law
	Accounting Standards
	Review Board
Main company types	Public companies (Ltd)
	Proprietary companies (Pty)
Main exemptions	Certain proprietary companies exempted from audit and publication
Stock valuation	LIFO not allowed
	Lower of cost and NRV
Fixed assets	May be revalued
Tax influence	Small
R&D	Generally expensed
Start-up costs	May be capitalised, amortised over up to five years
Finance leases	Capitalised
Contracts	Percentage of completion method
Groups	Associated companies included by note
Merger accounting	Not allowed

BELGIUM

Feature	Practice
Law	Roman
Main rule-makers	Company law
	Accounting *plan*
Main company types	SA/NV, Sàrl/BV
Main exemptions	Small Sàrl/BV exempted from audit and publication
Stock valuation	LIFO not allowed
	Lower of cost and market
Fixed assets	No revaluation
Tax influence	Considerable (e.g. depreciation)
R&D	May be capitalised and amortised
Start-up costs	May be capitalised, amortised over up to five years
Finance leases	Some leases capitalised
Contracts	Generally, completion method
Groups	Goodwill capitalised
Merger accounting	Not used
Other points	Legal reserve of 10% of share capital

CANADA	
Feature	**Practice**
Law	English
Main rule-makers	Business Corporations Act
	Canadian Institute
Main company type	Corporation
Main exemptions	Only public and other large companies must file
	and have audits
Stock valuation	LIFO allowed, but not for tax
	Usually, lower of cost and NRV
Fixed assets	Revaluation allowed
Tax influence	Small
R&D	Can be capitalised
Start-up costs	Not usually capitalised
Finance leases	Capitalised
Contracts	Percentage of completion method common
Groups	Goodwill capitalised, amortised over up to 40
	years
Merger accounting	Rare
Other points	Quarterly reporting for public companies

FRANCE

Feature	Practice
Law	Roman
Main rule-makers	Company law Accounting *plan*
Main company types	Société anonyme (SA)
	Société à responsibilité limitée (Sàrl)
Main exemptions	Abridged accounts for small private companies
Stock valuation	LIFO not allowed
	Lower of cost and NRV
Fixed assets	Revaluation (tax exempt) in 1978
Tax influence	Considerable (e.g. depreciation), but can be reduced In group accounts
R&D	Can be capitalised and amortised over up to five years
Start-up costs	As for R&D
Finance leases	Not capitalised, except by some groups in consolidated accounts
Contracts	Usually completed contract method
Groups	Proportional consolidation for joint ventures
	Mixed goodwill treatments
Merger accounting	Rare
Other points	Legal reserve of 10% of share capital
	Quarterly reporting by listed companies

GERMANY

Feature	Practice
Law	Roman
Main rule-makers	Company law
Main company types	Aktiengesellschaft (AG)
	Gesellschaft mit beschränkter Haftung (GmbH)
Main exemptions	Small GmbHs exempt from audit and filing
Stock valuation	LIFO allowed
	Replacement cost may be used if lower than cost
Fixed assets	No revaluations
Tax influence	Considerable (e.g. depreciation)
R&D	Not capitalised
Start-up costs	Can be capitalised
Finance leases	Not capitalised
Contracts	Completion method usually
Groups	Complex goodwill calculation
Merger accounting	Rare
Other points	Interim reporting rare
	Temporal method of currency translation usual

ITALY	
Feature	**Practice**
Law	Roman
Main rule-makers	Company law
	Principi Contabili
	CONSOB
Main company types	Società per azioni (SpA)
	Società a responsabilità limitata (Srl)
Main exemptions	Very different rules for listed companies
Stock valuation	LIFO allowed
	Market can mean NRV or replacement cost
Fixed assets	Revalued (tax exempt) in 1983
Tax influence	Considerable (e.g. depreciation)
R&D	Can be capitalised
Start-up costs	Can be capitalised
Finance leases	Not capitalised
Contracts	Completion method usual
Groups	Consolidation normal by listed companies only
Merger accounting	Rare
Other points	Legal reserve of 20% of share capital
	By mid 1990, the only EC country not to have implemented Fourth Directive

JAPAN

Feature	Practice
Law	Something like Roman
Main rule-makers	Commercial Code
	Securities and Exchange Law
	Business Accounting Deliberation Council
Main company types	KK (joint stock), YK (private)
Main exemptions	Only publicly traded companies need file
Stock valuation	LIFO allowed
	Cost, except NRV if lower for other than raw materials
Fixed assets	No revaluations
Tax influence	Considerable (e.g. depreciation)
R&D	May be capitalised and amortised over up to five years
Start-up costs	Not capitalised
Finance leases	Not capitalised
Contracts	Completion method
Groups	Only publicly traded companies need to prepare consolidated accounts
	Approximate temporal method used for currency translation
Merger accounting	Not used
Other points	Legal reserve of 25% of share capital
	Translated financial statements are also adjusted from originals

THE NETHERLANDS

Feature	Practice
Law	Roman, but in practice commercial regulation is more English
Main rule-makers	Commercial Code
	Accounting guidelines
Main company types	Naamloze vennootschap (NV)
	Besloten vennootschap (BV)
Main exemptions	Small BVs exempt from audit, allowed reduced publication
Stock valuation	LIFO allowed
	Lower of cost and NRV
Fixed assets	Revaluation fairly common
Tax influence	Small
R&D	May be capitalised
Start-up costs	May be capitalised and amortised over five years
Finance leases	Capitalised
Contracts	Percentage of completion method usual
Groups	Associates treated by equity method even in parent accounts
Merger accounting	Possible, but rare
Other points	More Anglo-American and varied than continental neighbours

SPAIN

Feature	Practice
Law	Roman
Main rule-makers	Company law
	Accounting plan
Main company types	Sociedad anónima (SA)
	Sociedad de responsibilidad limitada (SRL)
Main exemptions	Small SRLs exempt from audit
Stock valuation	LIFO not allowed for tax
	Market can mean NRV or replacement cost
Fixed assets	Revaluation (tax exempt) in 1983
Tax influence	Considerable (e.g. depreciation)
R&D	Can be capitalised
Start-up costs	Can be capitalised
Finance leases	Not capitalised
Contracts	Completion method usual
Groups	Consolidation not required until 1991 year-end
Merger accounting	Unknown
Other points	Legal reserve of 20% of share capital

UK	
Feature	**Practice**
Law	English
Main rule-makers	Company law
	Accounting Standards Board
Main company types	Public company (PLC)
	Private company (Ltd)
Main exemptions	Small private companies exempt from some publication
Stock valuation	LIFO not allowed
	Lower of cost and NRV
Fixed Assets	Revaluation fairly common
Tax influence	Small
R&D	Can be capitalised
Start-up costs	Not capitalised
Finance leases	Capitalised
Contracts	Percentage of completion method
Groups	Goodwill written off to reserves
Merger accounting	Possible; but fairly rare
Other points	Investment properties not depreciated

USA	
Feature	**Practice**
Law	English
Main rule-makers	Financial Accounting Standards Board
	Securities and Exchange Commission
Main company type	Corporation
Main exemptions	Only SEC-registered companies have mandatory audit and filing
Stock valuation	LIFO common
	Lower of cost and replacement cost
Fixed assets	No revaluation
Tax influence	Small (except with LIFO)
R&D	Not capitalised
Start-up costs	Not capitalised
Finance leases	Capitalised
Contracts	Percentage of completion method
Groups	Goodwill amortised over up to 40 years
Merger accounting	Fairly common
Other points	Parent company statements not available

INDEX